Preaching Biblically

Preaching Biblically

EDITED BY
Don M. Wardlaw

THE WESTMINSTER PRESS
Philadelphia

Scripture quotations from the Revised Standard Version of the Bible are copyrighted 1946, 1952, © 1971, 1973 by the Division of Christian Education of the National Council of the Churches of Christ in the U.S.A., and are used by permission.

Book Design by Dorothy Alden Smith

Published by The Westminster Press ®
Philadelphia, Pennsylvania

PRINTED IN THE UNITED STATES OF AMERICA
9 8 7 6 5 4

Grateful acknowledgment is made for use of copyrighted material:

Alfred A. Knopf, Inc., for the poem "Anecdote of the Jar." Reprinted from *The Collected Poems of Wallace Stevens.* Copyright 1923 and renewed 1951 Wallace Stevens.

Viking Penguin, Inc., for selections from Judith Guest, *Ordinary People.* Copyright © 1976 by Judith Guest.

Library of Congress Cataloging in Publication Data

Main entry under title:

Preaching biblically.

Includes bibliographical references.
1. Preaching. 2. Bible—Homiletical use. 3. Sermons, American. I. Wardlaw, Don M. (Don Mark), 1932–
BV4211.2.P735 1983   251   83–1276
ISBN 0–664–24478–5 (pbk.)

Contents

Contributors

DON M. WARDLAW, *editor*

Presbyterian; Professor of Preaching and Worship, McCormick Theological Seminary, Chicago, Illinois; preacher on the Protestant Radio Hour; past president of The Academy of Homiletics; one of his sermons chosen as one of the best sermons in a recent publication of sermons from the thirty-seven-year history of The Protestant Radio Hour.

RONALD J. ALLEN

Disciples; served a Christian Church congregation in Nebraska before assuming duties in 1982 as Professor of New Testament and Preaching at Christian Theological Seminary, Indianapolis, Indiana.

WILLIAM J. CARL III

Presbyterian; Professor of Worship and Preaching at Union Theological Seminary in Virginia; contributor to the Proclamation series, exegetical helps for lectionary passages.

THOMAS G. LONG

Presbyterian; recently elected Professor of Worship and Preaching at Princeton Theological Seminary, Princeton, New Jersey.

CHARLES RICE

United Church of Christ; Professor of Homiletics at The Theological School, Drew University, Madison, New Jersey; editor of *Word and Witness,* weekly homiletical and liturgical helps for lectionary passages; one of the authors of *Preaching the Story.*

GARDNER TAYLOR

Baptist; pastor of the Concord Baptist Church of Christ in Brooklyn, N.Y.; guest teacher of homiletics at Colgate Rochester Divinity School, Rochester, N.Y., Union Theological Seminary in New York, and Yale Divinity School, New Haven, Connecticut; recent Beecher Lecturer at Yale Divinity School, a series of lectures on preaching.

THOMAS H. TROEGER

Presbyterian; Professor of Homiletics, Colgate Rochester Divinity School, Rochester, New York; prolific writer, poet; most recent book on preaching, *Creating Fresh Images for Preaching: New Rungs for Jacob's Ladder.*

Introduction
The Need for New Shapes

Don M. Wardlaw

Preaching has long been indebted to discursive rhetoric for its shape and style. Recent theological changes have made it possible to see how preaching since the second century has been clothed mostly in prosaic dress. Prior to that time the controlling structure of Christian preaching was narrative, the recollection of what God in Christ had done, was doing, would do to intervene graciously in human affairs.[1] Reflection on the implications of that story for its hearers followed, usually in the form of exhortations and combined the synagogue's tradition of interpreting Scripture with pleas for behavioral change. The preacher concentrated on re-creating holy history, intermixing the recital with the "now, therefore," of ethical demand. Narration regulated sermon design. Reflection, application, and impassioned exhortation took their places along the story line.

When the church moved solidly into the Hellenistic world to offer the gospel, however, preaching adopted a discursive style that only now is being seriously reconsidered. In contrast to first-century narrative preaching, reflection became the basic sermon framework in the second century. Narration was confined to pauses for illustrations or allusions in the line of argument. Such an adherence to the prosaic quite naturally manifested the influence of Greek philosophy and rhetoric. Church fathers from Origen to Chrysostom, while imbued with the mind of Christ, exegeted and preached with the mind of Plato and Aristotle. To these Christians words of Scripture served more as symbols to be decoded than as unique conveyers of a holy drama. In most cases a philosophical mind-set given to search for higher meanings reduced the breath and eventfulness of Scripture to a still-life portrait begging for allegorical interpretation. The fathers preached these interpretations with a rhetoric that Greeks over the centuries had developed into a science of persuasion. Sermon shapes ranged from the less formal Stoic diatribe (learned discussion) to the elaborate panegyric (extravagant public eulogy). Whether by the terse Attic form or the pompous Asiatic style, preachers from Origen to Chrysostom structured their sermons by carefully reasoned argument.[2] The sophistic style, with its careful patterning of rhetorical questions, exclamations, contrasts and exaggerations, all clothed in a prolixity of images and metaphors, firmly established preaching as an act of persuasion through the medium of reflection.

The subsequent history of preaching, for all its complexity and diversity, bears one remarkable constant: the reflective shape of the sermon. Sometimes, with the medieval Schoolmen or the post-Reformation dogmatists, the sermon became an exercise in reasonableness, a discourse in theological refinement that by today's standards appears dry and dull. At other times, with Luther or Calvin, preaching assumed a commonsense air, beginning with a simple explanation of Scripture, followed by appropriate applications to daily life. But whether the mode was passion, tedium, or simplicity, the appeal almost inalterably rested on the framework of argument. Regardless of changing theologies and varying cultures through the centuries, preaching mostly assumed a debater's stance. One notable exception, however, is black preaching, structured more on the lines of the biblical narrative, probing the depths by appealing more to drama than to logic.[3] But for most preachers in the Western tradition, the case for Christ in preaching has been a case in court, as if *logos* were *apologia*. Preaching, per se, has meant marshaling an argument in logical sequence, coordinating and subordinating points by the canons of logic, all in a careful appeal to the reasonable hearer. To use Tom Long's image from his upcoming discussion, argument has served as the mold into which the gelatin of sermon content was invariably poured.

In the twentieth century most American preachers of Aryan descent have modeled their preaching on the sermon as argument. They have followed the masterful examples of such preachers as George Buttrick, James Cleland, Harry Emerson Fosdick, Gerald Kennedy, Robert McCracken, David Read, Paul Scherer, and Edmund Steimle. The reader, no doubt, will have other names to add to this sterling list. These are preachers who artfully and incisively labored to proclaim the gospel relevantly (and "revelantly," to anticipate Gardner Taylor's chapter) in the mid-twentieth century. Still, however persuasive these well-known preachers, their sermons worked from the assumption that the normative sermon form should be discursive. The sermon, to these men, is an oral essay with thoughts well grounded in biblical truth. All flights of the imagination, whether in story form, metaphor, or literary allusion, are carefully held in subservience to reflection. Narration itself is allowed to work only within the carefully defined limits of the anecdote, the historical allusion, or the illustration enlisted to make a point or to win the argument. Occasional departures from this norm into first person narratives, parables, similes, or stories have merely proven the rule. Many preachers choose the story form, the fantasy, or the eyewitness account now and then merely to break the monotony or to have fun. Some preachers josh each other about the three-points-and-a-poem form, as if a dash of poetry represents a flickering attempt to relieve the sameness of the argument. They laugh about or playfully dance around this Cartesian grid because they apparently have few other defenses against its dominance. The Greeks have stolen into homiletical Troy and still reign.

How aware preachers are of this intrusion and dominance is another question. Preachers have simply been grooved in the apparently timeless assumption that preaching as such seems to mean finding sensible, orderly things to say *about* scriptural texts, rather than letting those texts say things their own way. Of course, the logical, orderly way of expression may well be the way certain texts unfold themselves, the way certain texts need to be preached. Even so, most preachers assume that all texts, whatever their shape, ask to be presented in the garb of rational discourse.

Further, the vast majority of the people in the pews have been conditioned over the centuries to expect to "come and reason together" when the pastor mounts the pulpit. The weight of preaching tradition is pitted against sermons being regularly shaped any other way. How easily preachers, even newly sensitized ones, can work free from that weight remains to be seen. One is not surprised, therefore, when preachers take to their desks each week to construct more and more arguments. Still, T. S. Eliot catches the irony of it: "Hold tight, hold tight, we must insist that the world is what we have always taken it to be."[4]

Even when pastors admit their entrenchment in discursive rhetoric, they do not necessarily imply by such a confession that theirs is a harmful habit. In fact, many preachers assume that the habit is beneficial. Evidence can be called to testify that the sermon as argument has served worthily through the centuries as a vehicle for God's life-changing, culture-transforming Word. Many preachers naturally might wonder why such a time-honored instrument needs changing now. Surely no time seems more needful of clear thought and common sense than the present. The shape of preaching is open to radical reorientation now, however, simply because the transformed sensibilities resulting from cultural shifts through the twentieth century no longer give wholesale sanction to the assumptions underlying the argument form. When in earlier centuries preachers spoke Sunday after Sunday through one argument after another, they presumed that the preferred vehicle of oral expression from the pulpit was rational discourse. They took for granted that the reflective stance supposedly helped them keep a degree of personal distance in delivery as a sign of the objectivity inherent in their reasonableness. Argument also appeared the best way to impress the hearer. John Broadus, whose homiletical textbook set the standards for seminary preaching courses from the 1870s through the 1950s, wrote: "Argument, therefore, . . . forms a very large and very important element in the materials of preaching. . . . There are many whose religious affections and activity might be not a little quickened by convincing and impressive proofs that [Christian teachings] are so."[5] Broadus worked from the then uncontested premise that will

is the obedient servant of reason. Hence, once the preacher convinces the hearers of the "reasonable way," then the hearer's will
power automatically sets out to lead the hearer along that way.

These assumptions about the shape of the sermon, and the
hearers' capacity to appropriate that sermon, however, cannot
remain unchallenged today. Granted, all congregations need guidance in clear thought in order to remain faithful to the gospel. Even
so, reflection as the dominant sermon form may prove less a robe
than a straitjacket for the Word of God. In Scripture the Word
comes through a wealth of literary forms: metaphors, parables,
allegories, myths, visions, hymns, doxologies, oracles, correspondence, tropes, poetry, sagas, proverbs, diaries, biographies, au-
tobiographies, and history. Fred Craddock wisely asks, "Why
should the multitude of forms and moods within biblical literature
. . . be brought together in one unvarying mold, and that copied
from Greek rhetoricians of centuries ago?"[6] In short, beware of
Greeks bearing gifts.

James Thurber once said the trouble with books about humor
is they get it down and break its arm. Too many sermons get
scriptural texts down and break their arm rather than allowing the
text, like humor, to be itself *in its own medium*. "Every text wants
to speak for itself," insists Gerhard von Rad.[7] As Charles Rice says
in his chapter in this volume, "What we look for in homiletics
today are forms for the gospel that derive from what the gospel
is, how it is communicated, and what God in Christ intends for
our specific human communities." To put it Ron Allen's way,
"Each text has its own design, and we live in it according to the
type of space it is." To do otherwise with sermon shapes, Allen
points out, is something like covering the cathedral at Chartres
with vinyl siding.

Jesus' parables, for instance, were not designed for the acid
bath of criticism in which they are periodically immersed by each
generation of interpreters. Paul Ricoeur warns against dissecting
these similes, isolating their parts and deriving abstractions from
them.[8] Prior to the advent of form and tradition criticism, preachers in the Aryan stream of history have not enjoyed the freedom
to trust Scripture's indigenous forms to offer clues about how to

preach the Word those forms embody. Instead, most preachers have been trained to force a straitjacket of deductive reason over metaphors, similes, parables, narratives, and myths which in effect restrains rather than releases the vitality of these forms. When preachers feel they have not preached a passage of Scripture unless they have dissected and rearranged that Word into a lawyer's brief, they in reality make the Word of God subservient to one particular, technical kind of reason. The straitjacket of careful reflection becomes itself the message that Scripture's primitive materials do not seem communicable in and of themselves. "If theology becomes overly abstract, conceptual and systematic," warns Sallie McFague TeSelle, "it separates thought and life, belief and practice, words and their embodiment."[9] So with preaching.

Sermon as argument so often becomes the third party that breaks up the marriage of form and content in Scripture. To use Gardner Taylor's striking phrase, the text is "tortured out of its original integrity." Scripture is reduced to the object of a preacher's probe, with narratives, metaphors, and other such forms isolated in order to get at the "meanings they clothe." The careful argument, therefore, often makes the Word subservient to reasonableness. Worse, as Tom Troeger will point out in his chapter, "Focusing on the message that we have extracted from the passage, we can escape an encounter with the Word who is greater than all the print in our Bibles and all the pronouncements from our pulpits. We become gnostics, thinking we are saved by our knowledge rather than our faith." Ultimately, however, the preacher's insensitivity to sermon form makes Scripture the loser. The natural vitality of the Word in Scripture, expressing itself through its native setting and forms, is seriously hampered in its movement by the robes of the church's subsequent discourse. William Carl sums it up succinctly: "Structural problems in preaching inhibit the communication of the gospel."

Sermon as argument is just as much a straitjacket for the preacher as it is for the Word of Scripture. The necessity each week of making Scripture produce well-ordered truths severely restricts the preacher's imagination. As Fred Craddock puts it,

"David is trying to fight in Saul's armor."[10] Eric Heller tells a delightful parable about Valentine the clown who keeps looking for his lost house key under the street light. Valentine's friend, noting that the key is actually lying by the ash can over in the dark, asks why Valentine doesn't look for the key by the ash can. Valentine replies, "Because the street light isn't over there."[11] Homiletical tradition, comfortably ensconced for three hundred years in an empiricist culture, long ago tempted preachers to believe the key to unlocking biblical revelation is to be found under the light of rational analysis. Hence, most preachers relegated imagination to the menial task of searching for quotations and illustrations that merely embellish the argument. Suppose, on the other hand, that the preacher's imagination were freed to shape the sermon by the drama and linguistic power of the passage itself, establishing the movement of the sermon on lines other than the structures and movement of careful reason alone. Suppose the preacher's imagination were released to enable the drama or reality in a passage of Scripture to come alive in such a way as to involve the hearers more deeply and profoundly. Whatever its excesses in exegesis, traditional black preaching has always liberated the imagination to let the sermon find its flow from the dramatic flow of Scripture. For many other preachers this new and more fundamental role of imagination in preaching could turn a dreary task into a creative challenge.

The straitjacket of argument also often hinders the preacher's expression in delivery. An actor once remarked to a pastor, "We actors speak of imaginary things as if they were real; you preachers speak of real things as if they were imaginary." Good actors speak their lines in the flow of dramatic action, with a naturalness that belongs to "the world of darning and the eight-fifteen." Many preachers, however, speak more from a grid than a flow, more from dry discourse than eventfulness. They have little drama or imagery in their sermons to capture their imagination and liven their delivery. The detachment that marks their delivery stems less from the rhetorical intention of objectivity than from the difficulty of groping after abstractions. Charles Rice has shown what many have long suspected: that a preacher's delivery lights up with

expression when the preacher tells stories.[12] The dramatic movement of a story entices and elicits the expression of its teller.
Stories are propelled by their own power. Abstractions, however,
frequently stagger under their own weight. When they go any-
where in sermon delivery they have to be carried there.

The sermon as argument that restricts both Word and preacher
also frequently stands in its own way in moving the hearer. Hearers are moved toward behavioral change when they sense that the
speaker walks their streets and shares their visions. The preacher's
ordered and coherent argument offers no guarantee in itself that
the speaker is familiar with the realities of the hearers' lives. Surely
unity and clarity belong to good sermons of any form. Still, Leander Keck's concern about the pitfalls of standard sermon form
needs a special hearing:

> The clearly wrought sermon seems to imply that truth is rational,
> consistent, and reducible to limited number of points. This, however,
> seems to confer an aura of unreality to the sermon. The clearer and
> simpler the sermon the more artificial it may seem. This is because,
> instinctively, many persons believe that truth is glimpsed momentar-
> ily and in fragments, that it lacks symmetry, that it is awkward and
> angular as it breaks through to us.[13]

Again, medium as message does not jibe with experience as message. What kind of shape need a sermon take that by its form
seems to breathe the air people breathe and embrace the satisfac-
tions and shocks that people embrace?

In recent years students of the nature of language have declared
war on ways of talking about reality in rational abstractions. Implicit in the work of Paul Ricoeur, Philip Wheelwright, or Northrop
Frye, for instance, is the question whether or not one can nail
down things with words that dissect or categorize. Are words that
photograph more than portray, that isolate more than dramatize,
the preferred means for enabling the mind and spirit to touch upon
the profound, ever-elusive mysteries of existence? Says Wheelwright, "Meanings always flit mockingly beyond the reach of men
[*sic*] with nets and measuring sticks."[14] This recent discussion
about language makes more readily available some of the pro-

found values of poetic language. Wheelwright, for example, works with the helpful distinction between static and tensive language.[15] Whereas static language strives with semantic precision to eliminate ambiguity, tensive language risks ambiguity on the wings of metaphor, image, parable, fable, and simile, in order to create new possibilities for the reader or hearer to see What Is. Tensive language reveals through metaphorical expression the author's peculiar struggle in human experience. Tensive language arises from its author's personal journey into the hidden depths, turning to metaphor as the preferred means of carrying the reader or hearer along that journey. Such language refuses to be categorized or systematized in order to make positively clear what that journey means. Metaphors neither promise nor deliver such positivism. Instead, metaphors free the reader or hearer to put aside the objectifying pose and to experience reality in personal and suggestive ways. With sermons traditionally prone to use static language as their major currency, however, the air of realism suffers. The close argument does not necessarily prove to be that clear a window on reality. The hearer might agree intellectually with the preacher's reasoning, but still not feel sufficiently touched at the level of experience to try new behavior.

Students of language have also lost confidence in the capacity of argument to harness the will to its intentions. Established models for preaching presume that the hearer's will power stands at the beck of persuasive discourse. Rollo May offers needed perspective at this point:

> We inherited from our Victorian forefathers the belief that the only real problem in life was to decide rationally *what* to do—and then *will* would stand ready as the "faculty" for making us do it. Now it is no longer a matter of deciding what to do, but of *deciding how to decide. The very basis of will itself* is thrown into question.[16]

Philosophic tradition has long worked from the premise that reasonable actions flow from opinions, convictions, and motives in the same way conclusions rise from premises, principles, and axioms. Action, however, is not a species of argument; argument is a species of action. While logic participates in shaping motivation, it does not compass the subtlety, richness, and depth that give texture to a person's decisions to do anything. Jesus' hearers responded to a power and presence in his preaching that compelled allegiance on broader bases than logic alone. "Believing is not commanded by beliefs," writes Richard R. Niebuhr. "Beliefs come from believing; and believing is generated in experience."[17] If sermons are to move people significantly, today preachers need to understand that people are moved to action not by reason alone, and to seek new sermon forms compatible with that understanding.

Given the unsteady assumptions of sermon form as argument, Joseph Sittler's recent remark rings true: "Preaching is up for grabs today."[18] For that matter, all forms are up for grabs. The arts are experiencing an explosion of experimentation with forms that sends walls of tradition tumbling down. Twenty years ago the theater of the absurd and the *nouveau roman* by their forms challenged accepted perspectives on time and space, while cinematography over the past two decades has developed visual techniques that entice viewers into deeper fantasies. In painting, neo-expressionism is on the rise, relying, in the words of Hilton Kramer, "more on instinct and imagination than on careful design and the powers of ratiocination."[19] The contemporary German composer Hans Werner Henz in a lecture in 1963 summarized his attitude toward traditional symphonic forms when he said: "Today . . . we do not care to admit that these vessels are broken. . . . For the past fifty years and more, the symphony, as it was understood in the nineteenth century, has no longer existed."[20] Changing optics and transformed sensibilities demand means of expression that are no longer at home in yesterday's structures. Therefore, these cultural shifts sensitize the preacher to new possibilities for sermon shapes inherent in each scriptural passage. Argument as the dominant, singular sermon style looks more and more like a limited structure. When David Buttrick hails Fred Craddock's book, *As One Without Authority,* as "far and away the most exciting work on homiletics in some years,"[21] Buttrick's enthusiasm centers on the fact that Craddock is questioning the deductive analysis that structures most sermons. Homileticians are beginning to wake up to the cultural ferment over form and see with new eyes that preaching can take other shapes that carry new possibilities for hearers to experience the power and drama in God's Word in Scripture.

Most artists today work from the assumption that form and content belong in solution, that form participates indissolubly in the reality it represents. "Back of each poet's concept of the poem," writes Robert Duncan, "is his [sic] concept of the meaning of form itself; and his [sic] concept of form in turn where it is serious at all arises from his [sic] concept of the nature of the universe."[22] Nietzsche had this union of form and content in mind when he wrote, "One is artist if one experiences as *content* 'form.' . . . *From now on all content appears as purely formal* —our lives included."[23] Given this unity of form and content fundamental to perceptions today, the preacher can tentatively conclude that the form of the contemporary sermon necessarily works from union with its content, namely, the Word of God in Scripture. Rather than taking its cues from ancient or contemporary rhetoric per se, the sermon shape should derive itself from the content it seeks to embody and express. The passage of Scripture undergirding the sermon carries implicit signals for ways the sermon could form itself. Preachers open themselves to God's Word in Scripture, therefore, not only to experience the reality of God's gracious rule but also to receive some sense of how to re-present that reality in the sermon. Sermon form, then, becomes a hermeneutic in itself, releasing the scriptural Word among the hearers through the liberated expression of the preacher. Even so, the challenge still remains to determine, if possible, in what sense the sermon shape can participate in the Word it communicates.

Students of preaching have begun to struggle with this challenge to shape sermons by the Word. "The time has come," wrote David Randolph over a decade ago, "to brush aside tackhammer understandings of sermon construction and to test again the biblical soil for the forms of growth which are native to it."[24] Clyde Fant and Milton Crum likewise declare that the structure and movement of Scripture designate the structure and movement of the sermon.[25] Again, Leander Keck says preaching should "impart a Bible-shaped word in a Bible-like way," while Fred Craddock suggests that sermons need to adopt speech forms of the Bible rather than try to fit those forms to any other frame.[26]

So, then, the controlling question, what does it mean for sermon form to embody and express God's Word in Scripture? If preaching intends to reenact in the lives of preacher and hearers the saving acts of God in Christ as witnessed in Scripture, how does the preacher shape that reenactment so that it approximates as closely as possible Scripture's reality? The following chapters comprise the attempts of seven homileticians to answer these questions. While all contributors preach regularly, two of these authors were serving as full-time parish pastors when preparing their material: Ronald Allen as co-pastor of First Christian Church, Grand Island, Nebraska, and Gardner Taylor as pastor of the Concord Baptist Church of Christ, Brooklyn, New York. The remaining five writers teach preaching: William Carl, Union Theological Seminary in Richmond, Virginia; Thomas Long, Columbia Theological Seminary, Decatur, Georgia; Charles Rice, The Theological School, Drew University, Madison, New Jersey; Thomas Troeger, Colgate Rochester Divinity School, Rochester, New York; and Don Wardlaw, McCormick Theological Seminary, Chicago, Illinois.

The format calls for each writer first to wrestle with the question of sermon form from a theoretical view. Each contributor presents a perspective on shaping the sermon from the shape of the biblical passage. These varied perspectives about the hermeneutic of sermon form happen to fall into three distinct approaches (still, the tyranny of three's!). First, Allen, Taylor, and Troeger accent particularly the shaping of the sermon from the preacher's personal experience of the text. How the text encounters the preacher, appeals to his or her imagination and personal history, becomes the signal for lending a particular shape to the sermon. Secondly, Allen, Long, Rice, and Wardlaw concentrate on the experience of the faith community embedded in the text and see possibilities for structuring sermons from the shape of the human drama that gave rise to the text. Thirdly, Allen, Carl, Rice, Taylor, and Wardlaw see significant sermon shapes arising from the language of the text itself. Here the function and shape of the language provide possibilities for the function and shape of the sermon form. No contributor dwells exclusively in any one of these three categories. Yet each writer comes through with clear preferences and perspectives which, amid these three categories, add richness and variety to the discussion.

Each author then demonstrates his perspective with an exegesis and a sermon manuscript on a particular passage of Scripture. Hence, the proof of the pudding. The sermons come from a variety of genre in Scripture in order to demonstrate that creative possibilities for sermon shapes attend any text. Allen works from Jesus' parable of the Good Samaritan, while Carl moves with a Pauline exhortation in First Corinthians. Long deals with Jesus' cursing of the fig tree, and Rice with Jesus' proverbial sayings about material things in Matthew 6. Taylor and Troeger work with Old Testament texts: Taylor with the Chronicler's account of the death of Saul, and Troeger with Jeremiah's call to prophecy. Wardlaw responds to Luke's account of Peter's dream in Acts 10. In addition, each writer provides in the sermon manuscript a special running commentary that explicitly points out the reasons for moves or shifts in the sermon design. Here each contributor tries to be as practical as possible for the theological student or parish preacher, recognizing that all theoretical exploration of sermon form must turn for its final valuation to how the writer actually shapes his or her sermons.

In all, this book seeks to be more suggestive than definitive. The last word on the matter cannot be written. These chapters will succeed, however, when they start student and pastor on their way toward developing sermon structures more at home in Scripture and more vital for preacher and hearer alike.

NOTES

1. Three helpful volumes on primitive Christian preaching are: C. H. Dodd, *The Apostolic Preaching and Its Development* (London: Hodder & Stoughton, 1944); Robert H. Mounce, *The Essential Nature of New Testament Preaching* (Wm. B. Eerdmans Publishing Co., 1960); Robert C. Worley, *Preaching and Teaching in the Earliest Church* (Westminster Press, 1967).

2. Two helpful brief volumes for understanding the history of preaching are Yngve Brilioth, *A Brief History of Preaching* (Fortress Press, 1965), and DeWitte T. Holland, *The Preaching Tradition: A Brief History* (Abingdon Press, 1980). Note, further, these recent works on the history of preaching: William M. Pinson, Jr., and Clyde E. Fant, Jr. (eds.), *Twenty Centuries of Great Preaching* (Word Books, 1971); Edwin C. Dargan, *A History of Preaching,* 2 vols. in 1 (Baker Book House, 1954), and Ralph G. Turnbull, *A History of Preaching,* Vol. 3 (Baker Book House, 1974).

3. For an incisive volume on the history and nature of black preaching, read Henry H. Mitchell, *Black Preaching* (J. B. Lippincott Co., 1970). See also Charles V. Hamilton, *The Black Preacher in America* (William Morrow & Co., 1972). As Mitchell says: "Black preaching is as varied structurally as white preaching. Although there is probably a higher percentage of sermons preached by blacks in which the whole outline consists of the telling, at length, of a Bible story" (p. 178).

4. T. S. Eliot, "The Family Reunion," in *The Complete Poems and Plays, 1909–1950* (Harcourt, Brace and Co., 1952), p. 243.

5. John A. Broadus, *On the Preparation and Delivery of Sermons,* ed. Jesse Burton Weatherspoon, rev. ed. (1870; Harper & Row, 1944), pp. 167–168.

6. Fred B. Craddock, *As One Without Authority: Essays on Inductive Preaching* (Phillips University Press, 1974), pp. 143f.

7. Gerhard von Rad, *Biblical Interpretations in Preaching* (Abingdon Press, 1977), p. 18.

8. Paul Ricoeur, "Listening to the Parables of Jesus," *Criterion,* Vol. 13, No. 3 (Spring 1974), p. 20.

9. Sallie McFague TeSelle, "Parable, Metaphor and Theology," *Journal of the American Academy of Religion,* Vol. 42, No. 4 (Dec. 1974), p. 630. This article summarizes her subsequent book, *Speaking in Parables* (Fortress Press, 1975).

10. Craddock, *As One Without Authority,* p. 144.

11. Eric Heller, quoted by Robert Roth, "Reality and Metaphor," *Saint Luke's Journal of Theology,* Vol. 18, No. 3 (June 1975), p. 245.

12. Charles Rice, "The Expressive Style in Preaching," *Princeton Seminary Bulletin,* Vol. 64, No. 1 (March 1971), pp. 30–42.

13. Leander E. Keck, *The Bible in the Pulpit: The Renewal of Biblical Preaching* (Abingdon Press, 1978), p. 39.

14. Philip Wheelwright, *Metaphor and Reality* (Indiana University Press, 1962), p. 39.

15. Ibid., pp. 32–69.

16. Rollo May, *Love and Will* (W.W. Norton & Co., 1969), p. 15 (italics May's).

17. Richard R. Niebuhr, *Experiential Religion* (Harper & Row, 1972), p. 69.

18. Joseph Sittler shared this with me in a private conversation.

19. Hilton Kramer, "Art View," *The New York Times,* July 12, 1981.

20. From the program notes of The Chicago Symphony Orchestra, 88th Season, twenty-sixth subscription week, April 12–14, 1979, p. 27.

21. David G. Buttrick, review of *As One Without Authority,* in *Homiletic,* Vol. 1 (1976), p. 4.

22. Robert Duncan, in *Parable, Myth and Language,* ed. Tony Stoneburner, p. 41, quoted by Amos Wilder, *Theopoetic* (Fortress Press, 1976), p. 88.

23. Friedrich Nietzsche, quoted by John D. Crossan, *In Parables* (Harper & Row, 1973), p. 121.

24. David James Randolph, *The Renewal of Preaching* (Fortress Press, 1969), p. 100.

25. Clyde E. Fant, Jr., *Preaching for Today* (Harper & Row, 1975), pp. 110f.; Milton Crum, Jr., *Manual on Preaching* (Judson Press, 1977), p. 86.

26. Keck, *The Bible in the Pulpit,* p. 106; Craddock, *As One Without Authority,* p. 153.

Preaching Biblically

1
Shaping Sermons by the Language of the Text
Ronald J. Allen

FORMING THE SERMON

A building has a definite form. The form not only is functional but embodies a mood or a feeling. Standing in front of a cathedral, its graceful buttresses and delicate steeples sweeping toward the sky, produces a quite different feeling from pulling into the muddy parking lot of a white frame church at a country crossroads.

To change the form of a building is to change its character and the feeling it embodies. Many sanctuaries of the red-brick, county-seat churches in the Midwest, built at the turn of the century, had high vaulted ceilings outlined in dark oak beams, pews in a half circle so that wherever one sat, he or she had the feeling of being surrounded by a great cloud of witnesses. The pulpit, Communion table, and baptistery were together (architecturally and theologically) in the center of the circle. The wooden floors and stark plaster walls caused the room to echo slightly.

Remodeling seems inevitably to bring sheet paneling, a low, flat Celotex ceiling and an industrial carpet, with straight pews moved into two front-facing sections. The chancel is divided, and the Communion table is crammed into the narrow space between the two choir lofts, with the baptistery stuck onto one side (if visible at all when not being used).

Each of these styles of architecture embodies a different theology—and a different feeling. Remodeling is more than a matter of rearranging the nails.

The relationship between the form of a biblical text and the form of preaching from that text is much like that of a building and its form. Some texts are lofty spires, others are geodesic domes, and still others are shanties. Each text has its own design, and we live in it according to the type of space it is. I do not, for instance, sleep in the meat locker at the supermarket.

In this essay I explore the relationship between the form of the text and its meaning. A grasp of the nature of that relationship will yield important suggestions for moving from text to sermon.

A text takes its form from the pattern and structure of the consciousness of the author—or community—in which it was born. To follow that form in preaching is to communicate the text in the fullness of both its cognitive (discursive, rational) and intuitive (tacit, feeling) dimensions of meaning. To change the form of preaching to a form not clearly representative of the text is akin to covering the cathedral at Chartres with vinyl siding. If the text is a spire, then the sermon ought to be spiral in character. If the text is a geodesic dome, then the sermon could be spacious and warm. If the text is a shanty, the sermon might cause us to turn up our collars against the cold wind blowing through the cracks.

Language as Symbolic Medium

Because biblical texts (and biblical preaching) are expressed in language, I begin by taking note of significant recent developments in our understanding of the nature of language.

Language is a symbolic medium. Over the past sixty years, increasing attention has been given to the relationship between language and the realities it symbolizes. Writing from the perspective of the philosophy of language, and giving special attention to the relationship between language and conceptual process, Ernst Cassirer identifies two main, and very different, symbolic functions of language: (1) To "stand in" for something else; (2) To embody a reality in such a way that the reality can be fully apprehended only through its presentation in language.[1]

First, then, language can be used to "stand in" for something else. Robert Tannehill refers to this as an "informational" use of language[2] and Philip Wheelwright describes it as "stenic."[3] Paul Ricoeur speaks of it as the literal use in which the language means only what it explicitly says, and no more.[4] A word or a sentence or a paragraph or a book is simply a referent for something else, whether the other be a concrete object, like a pulpit, or whether it be an abstract thought. The sentence, "God is love," informs us about the nature of God.

In this use of language, there is a one-to-one correspondence between the word and the thing it represents. Especially useful in scientific circles, this use of language is clear and unambiguous, although Wheelwright points out that such language can lose its precision "when . . . the same words are repeated without examination or critical integrity."[5] Words and ideas are logically presented and connected, and to understand them one needs only a working knowledge of grammar and a dictionary tuned to the environment in which one is communicating.

In biblical interpretation and preaching, a consequence of using language in this manner has been to view the text, regardless of form, as a source of information or as a container of meaning, much like a plastic cup is the container of a milk shake. The purpose of exegesis has been seen as recovering the meaning—which is usually extracted in the form of a proposition, like "Jesus forgives sin unconditionally," or "God is on the side of the poor."

From this perspective, the purpose of preaching is to present the idea of the text in a clear and persuasive manner so that the listeners will agree with that idea and even appropriate it for themselves. Illustrations are just that: they illustrate the idea of the text. The preacher takes the passage (story, poem, letter, command), runs it through the mill of discursive logic, often in categories supplied by systematic theology, and boils down the residue like so much sorghum. The sludge of the form is thrown away.[6]

The second view of the relationship between language and the realities it represents—in which language actually embodies reality—is quite different. In this view, the sermon is seen as an embodiment of experience: as we enter into the "world" created by the sermon, that world comes alive for us in ways analogous to those in which the biblical text would have come alive for its hearers and readers. More than *hearing about* that world or having it explained to us, we *experience* it via the imagination.

When carefully and sensitively used, language can be, as Cassirer puts it, "no mere accidental cloak, but its [reality's] necessary and essential organ. It serves not merely to communicate a complete and given thought-content, but is an instrument, by means of which this content develops and fully defines itself."[7] Language does not lose its informational use, but can be seen to embody human experience, consciousness, feeling, awareness in such a way that the experience can be grasped only through the language itself.

Wheelwright describes such language as "tensive," because through it we readers or listeners experience the movement of the tensions of life—stretching and straining, releasing and relaxing. Through our participation in tensive language we (and our visions of life) are placed in tension with those of the text and stretched or stroked accordingly.[8] Wheelwright also calls this "depth language" because it communicates the depth of human experience.[9] Paul Ricoeur speaks of a second, "symbolic" meaning of a text. "Contrary to perfectly transparent technical signs, which say only what they want to say in positing what they signify, symbolic signs are opaque, because the first, literal, obvious meaning itself points analogically to a second meaning, *which is not given otherwise than in it.*"[10]

Robert Tannehill, building on the work of Wheelwright and that of literary critic Murray Krieger, finds that texts have an organic unity that "gives them a gem-like hardness. The text must be allowed to be the unique thing it is; it must be allowed to say its own word sharply."[11] The full meaning of the text is available only as parts of the text interact with one another. When it is treated as a whole, the text opens a window on the world.

In this view, the form of the text—its particular configuration of words, images, thoughts—cannot be separated from the meaning of the text, because it is precisely through the form that the fullness of the text's meaning is imparted. In this context, "meaning" includes that which is rational, cognitive, and discursive as well as that which is intuitive and emerging from the life of feeling. The form itself is an embodiment, an incarnation of meaning.[12]

Susanne K. Langer traces the relationship of form and meaning to physiological as well as philosophical and philological roots. She notes that the various modes of artistic expression (and, by analogy, texts) have a specific form because they reflect the form of the mental processes of their makers. That process, both conscious and unconscious, discursive and intuitive, has form.

At the level of raw experience, life is a continual flow of events, sense impressions, awarenesses (however vague), feelings, thoughts. Sometimes these are consciously experienced as well as logically connected and directed, but often they are intuitively felt, flashing and disappearing like fireflies in the night. All such processes make up consciousness. In the broadest sense, Langer notes that mental process includes *"everything that can be felt,* from physical sensation, pain and comfort, excitement and response, to the most complex emotions, intellectual tensions or the steady feeling-tones of a conscious human life."[13] Mental process is not static but alive, always in motion.

In her monumental work *Mind,* Langer says, "One may hope to describe mind as a phenomena in terms of the physiological processes, especially those which have psychic phases."[14] Literally, something happens in the self. "What is felt is a process, perhaps a large complex of processes, within the organism."[15] This process has form, albeit *living* form. Therefore, consciousness itself has structure and it is this structure which gives form to the text.

The living form of consciousness can be expressed because it can be projected into another medium.

What does it mean to express one's idea of some inward or "subjective" process? It means to make an outward image of this inward process, for oneself and others to see; that is, to give the subjective events an objective symbol. Every work of art is such an image, whether it be a dance, a statue, a picture, a piece of music or a work of poetry. It is an outward showing of an inward nature, an objective presentation of subjective reality; and the reason it can symbolize things of the inner life is that it has the same kinds of relations and elements. This is not true of the material structure; the physical materials for a dance do not have any direct similarity to the structure of emotive life; it is the created image that has elements and patterns like the life of feeling. . . . It seems to be charged with feeling because it expresses the very nature of feeling.[16]

A text as a form of experience, therefore, is not a photographic reproduction. Rather, a moment of insight and experience has been lifted from the random flow of consciousness and projected into another medium in such a way as to make a living representation of the author's awareness.

Moving from Ancient to Contemporary Experience

Many biblical texts may be understood as language used to embody meaning. They are images of living experience. People in the ancient world who were familiar with the rich depths—and utter paucity—of vocabulary, with overtones and undertones of feeling associated with a text's historical context and with the nuances of the contexts of the listeners, could experience the text's meaning directly. The ancient listener or reader encountered the text not by having it "explained" but by entering its world.[17]

> The form is immediately given to perception, yet it reaches beyond itself; it is semblance but seems to be charged with reality. Like speech that is physically nothing but little buzzing sounds, it is filled with its meaning, and its meaning is a reality. In an articulate symbol, the symbolic import permeates the whole structure, because every articulation of that structure is an articulation of the idea it conveys; the meaning . . . is the content of the symbolic form, given with it, as it were, to perception.[18]

When a work of art, or a text, is so perceived it speaks to an individual or a group at both conscious and unconscious levels.

When I go to the art gallery, I *look* at the paintings. Their meaning is given to me through the eye. When I go to the concert hall, I *listen* to the symphony. In the experience of listening, the symphony stirs me and my perception of life is enriched. I may not be able to state discursively the ways in which the symphony has moved me, for they may come out in the way I walk, or in what I feel when I read the news, or in how I respond to the fog in the morning.

Whereas an ancient listener or reader might perceive a biblical text directly, the historical conditioning of the text may make it difficult for a modern recipient to let the text speak directly to the senses. Indeed, even in the ancient period, when the experience of the texts and the experience of the people came to be strangers to each other, exegesis began.

The purpose of exegesis is to open the door to the world of the text so that we can enter it in ways that are historically, aesthetically, and otherwise appropriate.[19] The historical setting, the meaning of words, grammar, formal structure, literary placement, tradition-history, form and redaction criticism—all these deepen our appreciation of the text. But they are not the goal. *The goal of exegesis is to situate ourselves so that we apprehend the text as a living form.*

Preaching, guided by responsible exegesis, hopes to place the text and the listeners in such a relationship that the import of the text comes alive in discursive and intuitive dimensions analogous to those in which the text was alive for its ancient recipients. Preaching lets the world of the text shape our perception of our own world in ways that are historically, aesthetically, and otherwise appropriate.

If my text is one on forgiveness, I want my listeners to experience forgiveness through the medium of the sermon. If my text is one on judgment, I hope my listeners and I will experience being judged. If my text pictures eschatological hope, I want my listeners to experience a moment of glory.

By sharing imaginatively in such experiences, we will become better attuned to recognize them—and to respond to them with our whole selves—as they occur in the world around us. If I have lived in the world of the text through the medium of the sermon, then I am likely to reflect that world as I live amid jangling telephones, dirty diapers, the elders forgetting to make calls, inflation, and the threat of nuclear war.

The form of the sermon should respect the form of the text. By this I mean, not that the form of the sermon will necessarily correspond in a one-to-one fashion with the text, but that the sermon will manifest the characteristics of the text. If the text is a story, then the sermon will manifest the characteristics of a narrative. If the text is in the form of poetry, then the sermon will be poetic in character.

In some instances, the form of the text will directly shape the form of the sermon. A narrative text immediately invites the sermon to develop in the same pattern as the plot of the narrative. For instance, such an invitation is given by the story in which the hillsides around Elisha are covered with horses and chariots of fire which remain invisible to the armies of both Israel and Syria (II Kings 6:1–23). A natural form for the sermon is to follow the movement of the plot and to identify analogically with its characters. Who are the Syrians in our world? How are we like the king of Israel ("Shall we slay them?")? Have I had—*or can I imagine* —a comparable experience to that of Elisha and the two armies?

Other narrative texts may suggest experiences which the sermon would re-create for the congregation so that the congregation could analogously enter the world of the text. One dimension of the parable of the mustard seed (Mark 4:30–33 and pars.) is the experience of contrast between the expectation and the reality of the reign of God. Have I had—or can I imagine—an experience of such contrast?

One of the most pervasive and important characteristics of poetry is its reliance upon particular and concrete images and metaphors. The meaning of poetry is given to us as we participate in its imagery and in the movement of its metaphors.

Some poetry directly suggests a form and movement for the sermon. Psalm 102, for example, begins with images of despair.

> For my days pass away like smoke,
>   and my bones burn like a furnace.
> My heart is smitten like grass, and withered;
>   I forget to eat my bread. . . .
>   I am like a lonely bird on the housetop.

The psalm moves from such images to images of hope. Through participation in the images of hope, the ancient listener could have a momentary experience of release from despair and expectation of the new world (rebuilt Zion).

In preaching from the various genres of poetry in the Bible, we may want to use a contemporary image or images which vibrate in the same ways as their biblical counterparts. Where have I seen a picture of "comfort" like the renewed wilderness of Isaiah 40? Where have I seen a portrayal of judgment as trenchant and devastating as the locusts of Joel? Are there contemporary pictures that contrast two ways of life as vividly as Psalm 1: a tree planted by a stream of water and the chaff blown away by the wind? In a world in which flesh is sold like so many pigs in Omaha, where have we known the sensuality of the Song of Songs?

This approach is especially promising for those texts which are neither narrative nor obviously poetic, such as wisdom sayings, the various types of commandments, beatitudes, catalogs of virtues and vices—tracts which customarily are treated homiletically as "stenic" or "informational," with the major burden of the sermon being to unravel the application of the text and to deal with any difficulties.

The commandment "Thou shalt not kill," for instance, obviously applies to life. It serves to make the sermon more intriguing to struggle honestly with issues like war, capital punishment, or euthanasia. But ordinarily, stenic sermons take such texts as directed exclusively toward the regulation of behavior.

Suppose, however, we regard a commandment or a wisdom saying as an experience concentrated into the particular form of the text—as coal is concentrated into diamonds or lemon juice is concentrated into ReaLemon. What type of experience in the life of Israel could give rise to a commandment such as, "Thou shalt not kill?" How could it come to be regarded as divine revelation? What might generate a statement like, "You have heard that it was said to those of old, 'You shall not kill'; . . . but I say to you that every one who is angry with his brother [sic] shall be liable to judgment "?[20]

Simply to wag the finger and impose a command may be to place the congregation beneath a burden that produces only guilt and frustration. How different it might be if, in the sermon, we could create an imaginative moment in which the congregation could experience the brokenness caused by anger and the healing that can result from leaving "your gift at the altar." Instead of an impossible burden, the congregation is given an experience out of which they can live.

In particular, "prophetic preaching" can be strengthened by such an approach. Prophetic preaching often hopes for a change of social perception or (ultimately) for a change of life-style, both of which may be very threatening to a congregation. In place of slinging imperatives from the pulpit, we might reconstruct the world of the text in a sermonic world so that the congregation can *feel* what needs to be changed and why, and imaginatively "try on" what the changed world might be like.

Because texts of these categories come out of the human story, Gilbert Bartholomew has suggested that in preaching we sketch the stories out of which the texts came to expression, insofar as those stories may be responsibly reconstructed. The experience concentrated in the text would thus suggest a form for the sermon.

Robert Tannehill proposes that many sayings from the Synoptic tradition which appear to be discursive or informational may in fact be poetic in nature. They are not "general principles" or "commands," but "focal instances," radical instances of experience compressed into metaphor whose purpose is to jar the imagination in forceful ways to extend the text's implications into other arenas of life. In this way, the "command leaves room for the changing complexities of human situations and yet is able to help us in those situations."[21]

The crucial factor in new sermon shapes is that sermons reflect the second use of language, which embodies reality. One problem with preaching in this mode, of course, is that the majority of churchgoers still seem to think in the stenic, or propositional, mode.[22] Therefore, in our local congregations we will find it important to occasionally preach propositionally. But congregations can grow in their capacity to appreciate preaching in which the reality of the text is presented in a form compatible both with the form of the text and with the sensibilities of the listeners. Then, increasingly, the sermon can become a "world" for our listeners as the text was a world for its original receivers.

The Text / LUKE 10:25–37
EXEGETICAL OBSERVATIONS

Recent and widespread study of the story genre has stressed the continuity between human experience and its expression in the form of story. As we noted above, human experience is a constant flow of sense impressions, events, thoughts, feelings, and awarenesses, sometimes connected by cause and effect, sometimes randomly intersecting, while at other times passing like shadows in the night. Story takes its form from experience, with unnecessary and distracting details excised. The story form lifts from the undifferentiated flow of life a moment, an insight, or an image, and holds it out for our perception.

When we participate in the story by imaginatively identifying with the characters and the plot, our own experience and our own histories are deepened and enlarged and the story functions as a prism through which we find fresh meaning in other moments. Indeed, story may add dimensions to our experience that are more important to us than event in which we have been physically present.

Story can cause unfelt feelings to be felt. It can bring to life, or connect forgotten thoughts. It can cause radically new perspectives on situations as stale as the air in the attic. Through the medium of the story we can "try on" what life might be like from another perspective, much like that April Fools' Day when my spouse and I exchanged clothing, and she went to Newark in my charcoal suit (with maroon tie, of course) and I went to the library in a housedress. Even when the story is concluded, we live in its continuation, imagining how it might unfold in events and relationships around us.

Further, scholars now widely agree that the parables are to be apprehended as stories rather than as allegories or illustrations of a point, a lesson, or a truth.[23] Experience and the form of that experience, the parable, cannot be pulled apart like a banana and its peel. In order for us to grasp the parable, we need to enter its world and to follow its plot so that what happens in the story happens also to us. The parable then adds to our personal and communal histories and gives us fresh and intensified ways of looking at the world around us.

The most recent studies of the parables conclude that there may be more than one way in which to respond to a given parable,[24] for the nature of story is to contain several dimensions of meaning. In addition, interpreters come to the parable at different points in life, in different historical circumstances, with different expectations, and tuned to different needs—all of which may awaken different interpreters to different nuances in the parable. A runaway child reading the story of the prodigal son has a different frame of reference than the grandmother whose entire family lives within two miles.

To the ancient listener, the experience of hearing the parable would itself be revelatory. In the hearing of the story, the listener would experience the new reality or realities embodied by the parable.

The purpose of preaching on a parable is to re-create with the congregation the experience embodied in the parable. In language and imagery as vivid for the contemporary congregation as the ancient language and imagery was for the ancients, I want the sermon to re-create the world of the parable so that the congregation may enter it. The parable does not "give it to us all at once," but develops with elements of tensions, suspense, and surprise.

One of the benefits of the historical-critical investigation of the Gospels is the capacity to isolate (often clearly, but sometimes as through a glass dimly) levels of development within the Gospel tradition. In many pericopes we can find three layers of tradition with each to be interpreted differently: the text in its present use in the Gospel; the text as circulated prior to its present modification and placement; the level of historical Jesus. A preacher needs to be clear about which level he or she is interpreting, for each has its own peculiar thrusts. I encountered the parable of the Good Samaritan (Luke 10:30–35) in the course of preaching from the lectionary in which it is embedded in the larger unit (vs.

25–37).[25] Because the Gospel readings have been following Luke and because I have been preaching on the Gospel lesson at the redactional level, I will continue at that level.

Comparison with Matt. 22:34–40 and Mark 12:28–31, as well as review of form-critical and redaction-critical opinion, reveals that the parable itself (Luke 10:30–35) has been carefully placed.[26] The parable answers the question, "Who is my neighbor?" in much the same way that the formula of vs. 27–28 answers the question, "What shall I do to inherit eternal life?" We need to enter the context as one of Luke's listeners.

Luke's listeners would probably have identified with the lawyer (who was an expert in Torah), inasmuch as he was a respected member of the religious community. In preaching, I want to hear the parable, therefore, in ways analogous to the ways in which the lawyer might have heard.

From the perspective of first-century Jewish piety, the question of "Who is my neighbor" is the question of "Who am I required by God to help?" I am struck by the fact that Luke does not answer the question in the discursive mode, but instead tells a story. By entering into the world of the story, we are given a picture of neighborhood. The story, however, is not simply an illustration, as many of the commentators suggest, for when we enter the world of the story, we find that it does not answer that question at all. Instead, it creates an understanding of what it *means* to be a neighbor.

This insight unfolds only as the story unfolds. We are given it only as we are able to follow the process of the parable.

The setting is quite simple: robbers attacked a person (perhaps a merchant) of unmentioned national identity while that person was on the seventeen-mile road downhill from Jerusalem to Jericho. The road, rough and rocky, was known for such robberies, a detail that would be familiar to Luke's readers. The attack was severe, and our empathy is naturally evoked when we hear that the traveler was stripped, beaten, and left half dead.

It is helpful to remember how Luke's listeners, hearing the setting of the parable, would have expected it to develop. They could well have anticipated a triadic sequence of development, since that was a common feature of Palestinian storytelling. Hearing that the first person was a priest, they might have expected the last person (and the hero) to be a Jewish layperson, since the priest-hood was widely regarded as ethically and morally bankrupt.

A critical question, of course, is one of why the priest and the Levite do not stop to help the wounded traveler. While major interpreters are not fully agreed on why the priest and the Levite "passed by on the other side," I note that Lev. 21:1–4 was under-stood in the first century to say that if religious leaders had contact with a dead body, they would be declared ritually unclean. Fur-ther, they would lose their portion of the tithes and thus would be deprived of income. Therefore, avoiding contact with what ap-pears to be a corpse is both a matter of obedience to the divine will and a matter of survival.

In addition to helping my congregation understand the dilemma of the priest and the Levite, I want to help them understand the depth of hostility between Jews and Samaritans, so that they can experience the same surprise and offense as ancient listeners when a Samaritan emerges as hero. While this is a characteristic of the portrayal by Luke of the reversal of roles that occurs with the inbreaking of the reign of God, it would cause a pious Jew to choke. Who, in our culture, would arouse similar visceral feelings of disgust? Who is scum to us?

Finally, I want my congregation to understand the Samaritan and to experience what that character experienced. Although I am suspicious of finding too much in word studies, "compassion" is the only motive given for the Samaritan's stop. Since stories are carefully crafted, I turn to "compassion" *(splagchnizomai)* in the Bible dictionary and find that it is used, in part, to refer to the seat of feeling. To be compassionate is first to respond *in feeling* to the situation of another. Perhaps the Samaritan stops because of what he or she feels when seeing the wounded person.

As far as I can tell, the only clue as to why the Samaritan makes this response is the place of the Samaritan in ancient society, and the effect that may have had on the Samaritan. From the perspec-tive of the hierarchy of Palestine, the Samaritan is second best, someone only to be tolerated and taxed. The Samaritans may even have been outside the boundaries of Jewish responsibility before the law, so that if the person in the ditch had been a Samaritan, a Jew would not have been required to stop. The Samaritan had surely felt his or her sense of dignity and worth repeatedly impaled by first-century laws and first-century treatment.

Since I am a white, male, middle-class Christian, my situation is hardly parallel to that of the Samaritan. Nonetheless, I know what it feels like to have my ideas completely (and rudely) put down in a seminary. I know what it feels like to have someone so angry with me that the person leaves my church. I have a skin graft on my forehead, and I remember only too well how children would ask, "What's wrong with your head?"

The pre-Lucan parable ended with the question, "Which of these three proved neighbor?" That allowed the listeners to come to their own conclusions and to make their own applications. Luke completes the scene begun in 10:25–28 by having the lawyer affirm the story, but still leaves the listeners to unravel the implications in their own settings. Where is it, and how do they (we) go and do likewise?

Without meaning to be reductionistic, I can see that the parable has created a world in which the usual order of things is reversed. Indeed, in the parable, woundedness becomes a source of healing power.

The form of the text suggests the form of the sermon. I could tell a contemporary parable on the order of James Thurber, but a large segment of my congregation would miss the connection with the Bible and would thereby feel malnourished, even cheated. At the levels of both feeling and cognition, I want my listeners to experience the movement of the text from its initial question to wondering how, in our setting, and with what resources, we can go and do likewise. The journey itself is important. For by living in the world of the text, it becomes a part of my reservoir of experience and I can live out of it, wherever I am.

Sermon / WHEN THE UNIVERSE
HAS TWO CENTERS

The parable of the Good Samaritan is almost too familiar.
  Thumbtacked on the wall
    of a basement Sunday school room
      is the fraying picture:
        two empty sets of footprints,
        a person doubled up in a ditch—
          eyes looking up,
            questioning,
            tense,
              as two Samaritan arms reach out.
  "Go thou and do likewise."

The Good Samaritan is our example.
You, too, can be a Good Samaritan, and so
  the Christian Women's Fellowship is Good Samaritan
    when they make blankets for Child Saving Institute;
  the Christian Youth Fellowship is Good Samaritan
    when they walk for CROP*;
  I am a Good Samaritan
    when I stop along the road
      to help someone change a tire.
The Good Samaritan is our example.
We can be like him.

*Like many parables, this one has a long history of interpretation
in the church. Upon hearing the text, many listeners will feel
quite at home. "We know what this story is about." This is
precisely the position of Luke's listeners and readers. I begin,*

*Local examples reflect the life of our particular congregation of the Christian
Church (Disciples of Christ).

*then, as does Luke, with unsurprising, unthreatening common
ground with the congregation.*

We know this already as we come to the story in Luke.
　　We know this already as we hear of the lawyer
　　　　who has come to put Jesus on the spot.
　　　　　　Only, these are not lawyers who try cases
　　　　　　　　in the circuit court,
　　　　　　　　　　F. Lee Bailey types.
　　　　　　They are religious lawyers who interpret religion for the
　　　　　　　　unlettered of Israel.
　　　　　　They have been to Sunday school and have scored with
　　　　　　　　honors in Pastor's Class.
　　　　　　They have memorized the Ten Commandments,
　　　　　　　　　　　　　　the Golden Rule,
　　　　　　　　　　　　　　the Beatitudes,
　　　　　　　　　　　　　　the Minor Prophets in order.
　　　　　　They have served on the administrative board,
　　　　　　　　have been elected elder
　　　　　　　　　　or would like to be.

*I try to help us identify with characters in the story, as I think
Luke would have us.*

They are persons like you and me
　　who come to ask Jesus our question,
　　　　"What shall I do to inherit eternal life?"

*This question provides the immediate context of the story. It
needs to become our question.*

Who does not want eternal life?
　　Whether it be an ageless twilight
　　　　　　of shining haloes,
　　　　　　of fluttering wings,
　　　　　　of playing harps,
　　　　　　of picking fruit off trees,
　　or whether it be our own feeble attempts to hang on to

life, making it as eternal as we can
        with cosmetics and hair dyes,
        with diets and jogging,
        with writing chapters in books,
        with pension plans and IRA accounts.

In my congregation, the average church member still thinks of "eternal life" in terms of the traditional picture of heaven. I acknowledge that picture, but then suggest other ways in which our culture expresses longing for "eternal life."

I received a note from the Pension Fund last week.
  "Dear Pastor Allen,
  Only thirty-three more years until you retire. At that time, at your present rate of payment, your pension will be . . ."

My. I could live on that—forever.

I too am implicated. I, the preacher, therefore, stand under the word of the text.

Eternal life is not something we hanker for only after death.
We would have it now, if we could.

So we come to Jesus and ask our question.
  "What shall I do to inherit eternal life?"
    "You shall love the Lord your God
        with all your heart,
        with all your soul,
        with all your strength,
        with all your mind,
        and your neighbor as yourself."
  Eternal life: love of God and love of neighbor.
But the stakes are high.
So we press our question.
"Who is my neighbor?"
A certain person,
  nameless,

assigned to an eternal life of anonymity,
   driving around and around the mall parking lot,
   hefting in and out of the doctor's office,
   gliding in and out of the shadows of the night.
    The silent victim
      of tragedies we would rather not admit
        for reasons we would rather not know.

The sermon now follows the structure of the parable, with each element of the parable "contemporized" so that we are able to identify with its movement.

The traveler fell among thieves, robbers,
  who stripped him,
    beat him,
      left him
        half
          dead.

This is spoken very slowly and deliberately, with a final tone of voice.

He lies under the sun in shock;
  he looks dead—
    blood dripping and drying,
    mouth dry, scum forming,
    sweat running down his sunburned face into his cracked lips;
    stripped,
    helpless to cover his own nakedness,
    half dead but
  he looks dead.
Coming down the road is a priest,
  his clerical collar unbuttoned.
    A hard week at the church is finished,
      but now he is on the way to vacation,
        headed for Jericho's Holiday Inn
          to sit by the pool,
          to rub on Coppertone,

to drink iced tea in the shade of his umbrella,
to stare out the side of his sunglasses at young
women in bikinis.
For Jericho is a vacationland
every bit as much as
Cape Cod or
Catalina.
This minister is in no rush.
There is no church committee to chair.
No class to lecture on "love,"
no call pressing at the hospital.
His canoe is strapped to the top of his car, and he is
going on vacation.

*In most Sunday school discussions, the priest is berated for being
unconcerned, even hypocritical. This picture acknowledges that
common portrayal.*

Why doesn't he stop?

Long pause.

The Law.
The Book of Life.
"The priest who is chief among his people
shall not touch
or go into the room with
any dead body . . .
not even his father or his mother."
Unclean.
The priest who touches . . .
or comes near . . .
a dead body . . .
is unclean.

From the Holy Bible.
The Law.
The Book of Life.
And this nameless traveler looked . . . dead.
Is it worth violating the law of God

just to see if someone lying in the ditch is alive . . . or dead?
  Who can tell when a person is dead? Or alive?
    In the empty quiet of Intensive Care
     a body lies,
       its eyes never blinking,
        the only movement drops of glucose
          leaking from the plastic bag
           down the long, clear tube into the never-moving
           arm,
     life intelligible only by the
             beep,
             beep,
             beep
              of the monitor.
  And the priest has no monitor.
  Who can say,
    from across the road,
      "Alive"? or "Dead"?

*This image attempts to help us sense the priest's situation as a
genuine dilemma. It also helps us realize how much is at stake.*

Before I am too hard on the priest,
  I remember that I, too, am sensitive
    to expectations and feelings
     which constrain.
       As a man, for years
        I did not cry,
         not even by myself or for myself,
          or reach out to touch another man
          even when his guts were ravaged
          and he needed something more
          than a slap on the back
           and a sympathetic grunt.
   As a married pastor
  in a small community
    there are places I do not go—
      not alone,

not at night,
not because I am afraid of being clubbed,
  but because of what might happen
    to my ministry,
    to my spouse,
    to me,
      when the married pastor's car
      is seen at
        the single woman's home.

I try to illustrate concretely some "laws" that operate in our community.

Likewise a Levite,
  an assistant minister,
  a director of Christian education,
  a committee leader,
  a housekeeper of the Temple,
    he, too, passed by,
      perhaps with a reservation at Motel Six
        flapping in his pocket
          and the Law of God
            beating in his heart.
Then came a Samaritan.
  The Samaritan was different.
  A part of the difference between Jews and Samaritans
    was that the Jews believed
      that the center of the universe
        was the Holy City,
        Jerusalem,
          Mt. Zion,
    whereas the Samaritans believed
      that the center of the universe
        was a shrine just north of Jerusalem,
          Mt. Gerizim.

We are so accustomed to hearing the Samaritan lauded as the hero that we overlook the Samaritan's place in Palestinian soci-

ety. Historical details, lightly *sketched, begin to suggest how we might understand the Samaritan.*

Now to us that seems crazy.
  Who knows where the center of the universe is?
    Somewhere to the left of infinity?
But in that first-century world
  it made a world of difference,
    and the Jews had a headlock on Palestine,
      and anyone not like them
        was regarded as
          different,
          strange,
          almost diseased.
  In our twentieth-century world
    would it make such a difference?
      I heard someone say the other day,
        "If the Mexicans want to move to Grand Island,
          they'd better learn English.
        We don't need them old signs in Spanish cluttering
          up our rest rooms."
Well, where is the center of the universe?
Things got so bad
  between Jews and Samaritans
    that, a scant thirty years before,
      a band of Samaritans
        scaled the Temple wall in Jerusalem,
          slipped into the sacred spaces,
            knocked over the lampstands,
            scattered the Bread of the Presence,
            chipped their initials on the wall,
            and left a pile of
              dead
                human
                  bones.
        And that left the Temple . . . unclean.
How would it feel to you

if someone broke into our sanctuary
  threw a rock through the stained glass,
    carved an obscene gesture
      on the Communion table,
        and left in the baptistery
          a pile of fecal matter?

The attempt is for us to respond viscerally, as an ancient listener might respond to the Samaritan in the story.

Is it so hard for us
  to understand who the Samaritans were?
    Iranians?
    Russians?
    Blacks?
    Jews?
    Homosexuals?
    Child molesters?
  People so different
    that when we see them
      our bellies go tight,
        and without thinking
          we take a step back.
But the Samaritan stopped.
"He had compassion."
  Compassion, in Greek or in English,
    means "to suffer with,"
      to feel in yourself
        the pain of another,
      to remember enough of your own suffering
        so that you share in the suffering of another.
Maybe the Samaritan remembered
  what it is like
    to be wounded.

This is a major shift. Without glibly saying, "Even we lawyers have felt wounded," I hope for us to realize that we have, in our experience, resources similar to those of the Samaritan.

My first summer away from home,
   I was working down south in Atlanta,
      flunky in a big church.
They sent us down to Americus,
     where the clay is so red
        you think the earth is on fire,
           to work for a week at Koinonia Farm.
When we got to the farm,
     they soon found out we didn't know much about farming.
        I personally cut down a row of exceptionally strong weeds
          only to find out
             they were seedling pecan trees.
So they sent us out to paint a house
    which belonged to Miss Gussie,
       who had worked on the farm for twenty-odd years,
         and had been collecting Social Security
            for more years than I was old.
    But her house had never been painted.
When we pulled up in front of the
  gray
     weathered
       clapboard house
         we had the only white faces
          to be seen.
Perhaps we looked as nervous as we felt.
My first time to be the only white
   among a large number of blacks.
      My stomach was knotted.
      My palm was sweaty.
      My leg quivered ever so slightly.
Perhaps we looked as nervous as we felt,
    for when she came out of the clapboard house,
       wrinkled skin and cream-white hair,
         she put her arms around us,
           one by one,
             and up against her sweaty body

    I felt my stomach loosen.
After a while, my roommate Bob Drinkwater was on a ladder,
 his Co-Op hat turned bill-backwards,
 no shirt,
  a rag flopping out of his back pocket,
   massaging the house with his paint brush.
    You could almost hear the old boards say,
     "Thank you."
He came to a hole.
"Must have been some termite," he laughed.
 She was rocking on the screened-in porch.
The story came out like water from the faucet.
 She'd gone to cook at the farm.
  Big meals.
  And we knew they were good
   because she'd cooked one for us
    right there in her own kitchen
     with the fly-specked walls.
 But the farm wasn't welcome,
  not among most of the whites of south Georgia,
   precisely because it welcomed blacks
    and taught advanced methods of farming
    and made loans on new homes
    and blacks and whites lived on the same land
    and ate at the same table
    and used the same machinery for decades.
    Terrible stuff.
It was a dark night.
Moonless.
She was reading by the kerosene lamp.
A car came by,
 and then another,
  back and forth,
  back and forth.
A shout.
A curse.
Something her Baptist mouth wouldn't repeat.

And then a crack in the night,
   like thunder,
      only it wasn't thunder,
         and then another
            and another
               and another.

Pause.

Perhaps because she was black,
   and had gone to the back door of the restaurant
      and ridden at the back of the bus
         and received so many Christmas baskets,
            she remembered what it was like
               to be lying by the side of the road.
   And when she saw us standing in her yard
      acting as nervous as we felt,
         she knew what we felt like
            and put her arms around us.

*I am always reluctant to "draw out" the meaning of a story.
Here I simply try to make the connection between story and text
explicit as briefly as possible.*

And we?
Haven't we been wounded too?
After all, even lawyers are not vaccinated
   against the pain of life.
   Who can forget the feeling
      of standing by the open grave,
         the tent flapping in the breeze,
            wanting so much to hear the familiar voice
            but instead, hearing
               the snap of the rose
                  being broken from the spray
                     by the hand of the undertaker?
   Who can forget what it's like
      to open the closet door
         and see it half empty

for the first time?
Do I need to be reminded
of what it is like
to open a letter
and in the half-light of the hall
to read that I'm not wanted?
How many times did I see the blank stare
and hear the words stiff as briars,
"What's wrong with your head, kid?"

I try to suggest concrete experiences with which the congregation may be able to identify. I hope these images will help listeners recollect their own experiences.

If we can live by our memories,
perhaps we can be freed
to reach out hands and hearts,
not because we must obey a moral command
but because it is the response of life
from the Book of Life
and the One who came
to give us life.
And that's the story Jesus told
when some lawyers asked him,
"What shall I do to inherit eternal life?"

The biblical scene ends swiftly and gracefully. I try to end the sermon in the same way.

NOTES

1. Ernst Cassirer, *The Philosophy of Symbolic Forms,* 3 vols., tr. Ralph Manheim (Yale University Press, 1953–1957). Cf. his abbreviated treatment in *Language and Myth,* tr. Susanne K. Langer (Dover Publications, 1946), his *Essay on Man* (Yale University Press, 1962), pp. 23–27, and now *Symbol, Myth and Culture: Essays and Lectures of Ernst Cassirer,* ed. Donald Verene (Yale University Press, 1979), pp. 145–195.

2. Robert Tannehill, *The Sword of His Mouth* (Scholars Press, 1975), pp. 6–7.

3. Philip Wheelwright, *Metaphor and Reality* (Indiana University Press, 1962), pp. 16, 35.

4. Paul Ricoeur, *The Symbolism of Evil*, tr. Emerson Buchanan (Beacon Press, 1967), p. 15.

5. Wheelwright, *Metaphor and Reality*, p. 38.

6. Lest we judge such approaches too harshly, let us remember that the style of preaching in a given era often reflects the best understanding of the ways of human knowing and the best biblical exposition available to the homileticians of the time. In a time and place appropriate to it, for instance, propositional preaching has helped many pastors and congregations. Our obligation is not to "put down" others but to build upon the insights of our time as they did in their eras.

7. Cassirer, *The Philosophy of Symbolic Forms*, Vol. 1, p. 86. "Instead of measuring the content, meaning and truth of intellectual forms by something extraneous, which is supposed to be reproduced in them, we must find in these forms themselves the measure and criterion of their truth and intrinsic meaning. Instead of taking them as mere copies of something else, we must see in each of these spiritual forms a spontaneous law of generation: an original way and tendency of expression which is more than a mere record of something initially given in fixed categories of real existence" (Cassirer, *Language and Myth*, p. 8).

8. Wheelwright, *Metaphor and Reality*, pp. 45–46.

9. Philip Wheelwright, *The Burning Fountain* (University of Indiana, 1954), pp. 86ff. Wheelwright perceives that "depth language" can violate the rules of ordinary grammar and definition and often appears to contain more than one level of meaning.

10. Ricoeur, *The Symbolism of Evil*, p. 15. My emphasis.

11. Tannehill, *The Sword of His Mouth*, pp. 16 and 21.

12. To have cited these opinions is to have stuck no more than a toe in the rapids of literature flowing with this theme. E.g., consider a representative statement from the New Hermeneutic. "The primary phenomenon in the realm of understanding is not understanding *of* language but understanding *through* language . . . the word is what opens up and mediates understanding." Gerhard Ebeling, *Word and Faith* (Fortress Press, 1963), p. 318. Cf. Sallie McFague TeSelle, *Speaking in Parables* (Fortress Press, 1975), pp. 43–66; Amos Wilder, *Early Christian Rhetoric: The Language of the Gospel* (Harvard University Press, 1971); Norman

Perrin, *Jesus and the Language of the Kingdom* (Fortress Press, 1976).

13. Susanne K. Langer, *Problems of Art: Ten Philosophical Lectures* (Charles Scribner's Sons, 1957), p. 15. This is an excellent introduction to her thought as is her *Philosophy in a New Key* (Harvard University Press, 1957).

14. Susanne K. Langer, *Mind: An Essay on Human Feeling* (Johns Hopkins University Press, 1967), Vol. 1, p. 29. Cf. *Mind: An Essay on Human Feeling* (Johns Hopkins University Press, 1972), Vol. 2.

15. Langer, *Mind,* Vol. 1, p. 21. Other recent studies have sought to show that the halves of the brain perform separate functions: one half performs the rational/discursive/logical function and the other half the intuitive/aesthetic function. Each person thus has both "perceptual modalities," although they operate with different strengths in each person. Basic studies include Robert E. Ornstein, *The Psychology of Consciousness* (Viking Press, 1972); Kenneth Pelletier, *Toward a Science of Consciousness* (Dell Publishing Co., Delta Books, 1978); Eugene P. Wratchford, *Brain Research and Personhood* (University Press of America, 1979). For theological and homiletical appropriation of this way of understanding consciousness, see Walter Wink, *Transforming Bible Study* (Abingdon Press, 1980), pp. 17–34; Richard A. Jensen, *Telling the Story: Variety and Imagination in Preaching* (Augsburg Publishing House, 1980), pp. 123–126. The implication for homiletics is clear: preaching of the sort proposed in this book that engages both halves of the brain will speak to the full range of consciousness, while preaching which engages only one side or the other has power comparable to a four-cylinder car climbing Pike's Peak on two cylinders.

16. Langer, *Problems of Art,* p. 98.

17. Of course, in order to enter the world of the text, some explanation of now distant and archaic phenomena may be needed. But with respect to preaching, the explanation—even artfully done—is the servant and not the goal of exegesis.

18. Susanne K. Langer, *Feeling and Form* (Charles Scribner's Sons, 1953), p. 52.

19. I agree with much recent discussion that texts may have more than one level of meaning and that, indeed, they may be charged with meaning(s) unknown to ancient authors. It is sometimes possible for texts to speak to us without mediation. However, to disregard ancient context and reference is to open the door to wild flights of exegetical, hermeneutical, and homiletical fancy and to close the door on potentially enriching and enlivening knowledge.

20. In pursuing a question like this, a preacher must be guided by *careful* historical research and reconstruction.

21. Tannehill, *The Sword of His Mouth,* pp. 67–68. In his focus on literary analysis of the texts, Tannehill tends to overlook historical referents which could be enriching. The poetic character of the wisdom literature is now being examined afresh, see, e.g., *Semeia* 17, 1980.

22. This is supported by the research of James W. Fowler into cognitive operation. Note his *Stages of Faith* (Harper & Row, 1981), pp. 150–183, and James Fowler with Sam Keen, *Life Maps: Conversations on the Journey to Faith* (Word, 1978), pp. 60–79.

23. "Standard" guides, written from a variety of viewpoints, into the parables include: Kenneth E. Bailey, *Poet and Peasant* (Wm. B. Eerdmans Publishing Co., 1976), and *Through Peasant Eyes* (Wm. B. Eerdmans Publishing Co., 1980); Charles E. Carlston, *The Parables of the Triple Tradition* (Fortress Press, 1975); John D. Crossan, *In Parables* (Harper & Row, 1973); C. H. Dodd, *The Parables of the Kingdom,* rev. ed. (Charles Scribner's Sons, 1961); Joachim Jeremias, *The Parables of Jesus,* tr. S. H. Hooke, rev. ed. (Charles Scribner's Sons, 1969); Eta Linneman, *Parables of Jesus,* tr. John Sturdy (London: S.P.C.K., 1966); Pheme Perkins, *Hearing the Parables of Jesus* (Paulist Press, 1981); Dan O. Via, Jr., *The Parables* (Fortress Press, 1967).

24. Recent studies that highlight ways in which the parables manifest more than one level of meaning include: Madeleine Boucher, *The Mysterious Parable* (Catholic Biblical Association of America, 1977); John D. Crossan, *Cliffs of Fall* (Seabury Press, 1980); Mary Ann Tolbert, *Perspectives on the Parables* (Fortress Press, 1978); Amos N. Wilder, *Jesus' Parables and the War of Myths* (Fortress Press, 1982).

25. Series C, the Eighth Sunday after Pentecost.

26. In addition to appropriate passages in the studies listed in notes 23 and 24 and the commentaries, see *Semeia* 2, 1974, and especially Walter Wink, "The Parable of the Compassionate Samaritan," *Review and Expositor,* Vol. 76 (1979), pp. 199–218.

2
Shaping Sermons
by the Context of the Text

Don M. Wardlaw

FORMING THE SERMON

The Word as Address

Form and content, while classically treated as separate, ultimate categories, are viewed by contemporary society as a dynamic fusion in which meaningful form of any kind participates in the content it embodies. For the preacher, this means that a sermon's form should necessarily work in union with its substance, namely, the Word of God in Scripture. Hence the controlling question: How can sermon form embody and express God's Word in Scripture? This question assumes that the more integral a sermon's form is to its content, the Word in Scripture, the better chance that Word in Scripture has to be heard and felt by today's congregations. Such an assumption presupposes clarity about the nature of God's Word in Scripture and about how the preacher listens for that Word. A brief glance at these broader matters of interpretation is therefore necessary before we focus on the dynamics of sermon form.

God's Word in Scripture can hardly be called the "content" for preaching in the sense that water could be called the content of a glass. The term "God's Word" eludes such simple classification, for the very expression "God's Word" comprises in itself a dynamic fusion of form and content. In biblical thought the way God speaks and what God says form an indissoluble union. In the first chapter of Genesis, God's mere utterance becomes a creative act:

"And God said. . . . And it was so" (Gen. 1:6, 7, 9, 11, 14, 20, 24, 29, 30). The Hebrew word for "word," *dabar,* means both "utterance" and "deed." John gives central focus to this form/ content unity in the prologue to the Fourth Gospel when he declares, "And the Word became flesh and dwelt among us" (John 1:14). Goethe's Faust, wrestling with the best way to translate the opening line of John's Gospel, emerges with the confident conclusion that the line should read, "In the beginning was the Deed!"[1] In so concluding, Goethe has Faust correctly reflect the form/content fusion in John's use of the concept "the Word." The Word *does* what it says. The Word acts in a form inherently expressive of its content. When John refers to Christ as "the Word become flesh" he proclaims the incarnation as a unique, ultimate embodiment of the form/content union in the Word. The way God speaks and what God says dramatically come together in the incarnation.

God's Word, then, is God's revealing activity, God speaking through events to declare both the human predicament and the human possibility. Over a decade ago such biblical scholars as Ernst Fuchs and Gerhard Ebeling through their "new hermeneutic" helped interpreters see the Word not as the object of study but as the subject that addresses the interpreter regarding the human condition. In Scripture this Word as address occurs within the horizon of a narrative that comprises a drama of salvation for a particular Semitic people. In broad strokes the story shows God delivering this people from Egyptian slavery to become bearers of a covenant relationship first formed at Sinai and subsequently tested in the triumphs and tragedies of the Hebrew nation. The narrative climaxes in the ministry, crucifixion, and resurrection of Jesus Christ. At Pentecost the New Israel, the church, comes into being as the bearer of the new covenant in Christ to the whole world. Scripture presents this narrative through a tradition whose multiplicity of voices and genres stretches over a thousand years. Thus Scripture serves as a unique, multifaceted witness to this Word. To preach this Word in Scripture, then, is to shape sermons in ways coherent with the dynamic, multiform address of that Word.

Many biblical scholars asserted thirty years ago that to hear this Word aright the interpreter should try to move behind the people's *account* of the drama of salvation in order to enter directly into the ancient events themselves. These scholars assumed that the faith community's testimony veiled rather than conveyed the reality carried by the story. They also assumed that the goal of interpreting that Word was to return as closely as possible to the initial historical context in order to hear once more Goliath roar or to feel again the earth shake on Good Friday. Each pericope or passage supposedly contained enough clues to lead interpreters back through a twilight zone of the church's witness to the original setting of that Word—to David's actual prayer, or to Jeremiah's original oracle, or to Jesus' authentic work and words, or to Paul's precise pronouncement. In short, contextual interpretation presumed the context of the *original* historical events.

Thanks to recent form, tradition, and redaction criticism,[2] however, many interpreters now think that Scripture may not always provide enough evidence to lead with certainty back from the context of early witnesses to actual events themselves. For instance, Matthew's rendering of Jesus' parable of the Lost Sheep (Matt. 18:10–14) embodies a plea for the disciples' pastoral sensitivity, while Luke's version of the same parable (Luke 15:3–7) makes a defense against exclusivist Pharisees; modern scholars hesitate to assume with C. H. Dodd and Joachim Jeremias that some unembellished original version of that parable lies behind Matthew and Luke at the end of an interpreter's yellow-brick road. Instead, they assert that the witness to God's Word in that parable includes, rather than ignores, Matthew's or Luke's perspective and context. Today's careful interpreter resists looking past accretions or subtractions of biblical writers of the tradition in order to search for a primitive version that supposedly waits as buried treasure to be discovered. In Elizabeth Achtemeier's words, "It is the final shape of the canon, rather than the stages in its development uncovered by historical criticism, which . . . [defines] the text's meaning."[3] James Sanders explains further:

> The Bible comes to us out of the liturgical and instructional lives of
> the ancient believing communities which produced and shaped it.
> What is in the text is there not only because someone in antiquity
> was inspired to speak a needed word to his or her community,
> because that community valued the communication highly enough
> to repeat it and recommend it to the next generation and to a
> community nearby.[4]

Today's interpreter, then, sees God's Word as not so much hidden
behind the faith community's witness as borne by that context.
Therefore, rather than shelving the tools of historical-critical
study, the interpreter uses them to get in touch with the life of
those witnesses who give rise to the passage. The more a preacher
enters into the dynamics and flow of these communities' witnesses in Scripture to holy events, and the more he or she senses
the life of God's people that pervades the language and structure
of the passage, the more adequately that preacher can hear and
preach the Word of God embodied by that passage. In short, the
scriptural substance for a sermon should be cued by the context
of the faith community that evoked or wrote the passage. This is
what we mean by a contextual sermon.

The Contextual Sermon: A Case Study

A contextual sermon shape that works in union with sermon
content will reflect the faith community context as seen through
the language and structure of a passage of Scripture. Consider, for
example, a sermon on Phil. 2:5–11, one of the great Christological
passages in the New Testament. A traditional, discursive sermon
on this famous *kenosis* passage would likely present these verses
as a model of the humble obedience we all "must" have as
Christians. Such a sermon would be shaped as a point-by-point
demand for self-denial in the Christian community on the grounds
of Christ's self-emptying. But today's preacher, in addition to
questioning anyone's capacity to emulate Christ's self-emptying,
might also wonder how well such a careful kind of argument
conveys the Word as seen in Phil. 2:5–11. Is it not better to couch
the sermon in such a way that the hearers can experience—and
identify with—the life situation of Paul and the Philippian Christian

community that gave rise to this passage? In this way sermon form becomes significant[5] for sermon hearers today by helping convey the church's life in the passage.

In working with Phil. 2:5–11, the preacher begins by listening where possible for the human context that poses the question that calls the text into being.[6] The preacher seeks to feel the human drama that flows like an undercurrent in the pericope, to look between the lines for the situation that gave birth to the passage. The components that belong to that event or to those events are the author's intent, the hearers' mind-set, and the question being addressed. Some (notably Paul Ricoeur in his *Interpretation Theory*[7]) argue that the way to the understanding of a text is clouded when the interpreter tries to fathom the ego of the text's author or to draw inferences from the text's underlying history. But granted that the relativities of the author's mind and the original setting inevitably obscure to some extent the focus of one interpreting from a historical bent, can the interpreter, on the other hand, expect the language of the text alone to provide its own context for interpretation? How can one understand language apart from the community and life situation that gave it birth?

Recent thinking by such literary critics as Jay Schleusener or John Sherwood promotes a commonsense view of interpretation that sees author's intent, hearers' mind-set, and text integrally related and therefore necessary dimensions of understanding the text.[8] "I would prefer to say," writes Schleusener, "that the context of reading *is* a social context."[9] Schleusener also points out that the interpreter cannot recognize meanings in a passage without at the same time recognizing the community and its conventions that are borne by the passage. Likewise, Sherwood concludes: "If we were to grant that . . . the author's intentions are irrelevant, then the labors of critics and scholars are futile and much classroom activity wasteful."[10] The claims of Schleusener and Sherwood for the value of historical explanations in interpretation reinforce the conviction that the life situation of Paul and the Philippian church *is* the context for beginning to understand Phil. 2:5–11.

Let us apply the above, therefore, to Phil. 2:5–11:

The question raised is: How can these quarreling Christians be encouraged to make up and dwell in unity? The squabbling flock of Philippian Christians—Euodia and Syntyche in particular (4:2), but others as well who grumble selfishly (2:3, 14)—are by their dissension weakening the Philippian Christians' stand against their pagan detractors (1:28).

The fact that Phil. 2:6–11 is one of the primitive church's earliest hymns makes clearer Paul's intent in these lines.[11] Ostensibly, Paul fortifies his appeal for Philippian selflessness by quoting a hymn text that celebrates self-emptying as the core of the incarnation. But the preacher moves more deeply into Paul's aim upon seeing that Paul is singing more than contending. According to Luke as the author of The Acts, Paul has a habit of immersing his soul in hymns when he is in prison (Acts 16:25). Communicating from prison with pastoral concern for his quarreling friends, Paul shifts from prose to poesis at Phil. 2:6, suggesting the probability of a heightened feeling level in his concern. Paul was probably dictating this letter to the Philippians while under house arrest, pacing to and fro near his secretary. This hymn could well have moved into his consciousness as he pondered the kind of humility needed by these divisive Philippians. Amos Wilder senses this power of poetics when he writes, "We should recognize that human nature and human societies are more deeply motivated by images and fabulations than by ideas."[12] At this level of perception Paul makes his pitch for unity. He sings to his people the hymn he may well have sung with them often. With this change in language Paul conceivably elicits the sights and sounds of the worshiping Philippian community, creating an image more conducive in this particular context for altering consciousness than a closely reasoned argument alone.

Another important component that belongs to the question that brings Phil. 2:5–11 into being is the world view of the audience/hearers. Biblical scholars today stress the importance for interpreters to understand the mind-set of the people to whom the passage is addressed, in order to have an accurate sense of the reality in the passage.[13] Hence, with the miraculous catch of fish by the post resurrection disciples in John 21:1–14, the author of the

Fourth Gospel combats the implied mind-set in the Christian community at the time that the church without the earthly Jesus would net no souls for Christ. Similarly, with Jesus' story of the Great Banquet (Luke 14:15–24) Luke combats a world view that honors those who sit in high places and assumes that God's power and authority are exercised only on vertical lines. One attitude implied by Paul's use of this moving Christological hymn in Phil. 2:6–11 is the notion common to both Paul's world and our own that the only way to get ahead is to look out solely for number one[14]; or, as Paul describes the problem (2:4), where each "looks only to his own interests." With this hymn Paul reminds his readers that God exalts Him who emptied rather than filled Himself. Paul blows the whistle on a self-serving attitude that was beginning to dominate the consciousness of the Philippian Christians.

The interpretation now moves from the life beneath or between the lines of Phil. 2:5–11 to the reality held in the lines themselves. Here the form and structure critics, whose contributions in recent years have breathed new life into hermeneutics, help the preacher focus on three qualities in the language itself: form, structure, and tone.[15]

As earlier indicated, the *form* of most of this Philippians passage is a hymn, specifically six couplets used in antiphonal fashion, a common liturgical practice with the early church.[16] Paul evidently felt it more important to sing to his readers/hearers than to argue with them. His choice of form would predispose his audience's response. "Obviously," writes David Buttrick, "form tends to orient consciousness; it predetermines expectation."[17] On comes the clown in silent mime, for instance, and the audience gets set for irony. On comes the limerick ("There once was a man from . . .") and the hearers brace themselves for laughter with a fifth line's clever twist. On comes Paul echoing a favorite hymn, and conceivably something clicks in the minds of the Philippian Christians. Form, per se, has the capacity to function as subject in shaping the hearer's response.

While the form of Phil. 2:6–11 is a hymn, that hymn is *structured* to convey meaning for interpretation. First, the cluster of contrasts in these couplets—form of God/form of servant, form of God/human form, grasping/emptying, death on a cross/exaltation—loads the servant metaphor with irony, making this use of language a *skandalon* in itself.[18] The irony in the language of exaltation within abasement catches the preacher off guard because glory does not come that way in the world. The hymn's structure offers meaning, secondly, in its "parabola" or a-b-a design. The hymn's imagery begins in heaven (2:6), descends to earth (2:7–8), and returns to heaven again (2:9–11); a universal mythical shape. This structure offers a paradigm for obedience that begins with a vision of Christ's divine prerogatives, moves to Christ's surrender to that privilege in his descent into the human predicament, then swings back up to Christ's regained status through his exaltation. Here the shape of the hymn's story carries a message of the kind of self-sacrifice Paul says can restore unity to the divided Philippian Christians. In short, a-b-a is Christ's way. When the Philippian Christians sacrifice the prerogatives of status or power within their group in order to enter into the needs of others in the community, then God waits to exalt that self-sacrifice with unity just as God exalted Christ's ultimate self-sacrifice with a heavenly reunion.

The *tone* of a passage—that is, word choice and manner of expression—often significantly influences a language event by reflecting the feelings of the author/speaker. For instance, Paul's staccato burst of hard words in his self-defense in Galatians 1 makes clear his no-nonsense, confrontive mood. Similarly, Paul's tone in this Philippians passage that challenges squabbling Christians to unity conveys a warm pastoral concern. Even though the Philippians bicker, they are still to Paul "beloved" (Phil. 2:12). Feeling-laden words in 2:1–2, "love," "affection," "sympathy," "joy," and "accord," introduce his appeal for unity. Then Paul adds the hymn in 2:6–11, with its association of fellowship and worship at Philippi, to set a total tone that is at once conciliatory and gracious. The accent fits the overall mood of joy reflected in the entire epistle. The warm coloration itself becomes a message of acceptance. Paul comes to these divisive Christians, not with a sword, but with peace. This conciliatory tone would disarm his Philippian colleagues so that they might listen more openly to his plea for unity. As with any rhetorician, Paul counts on tone to do its own work on his behalf.

The work so far with Phil. 2:5–11 demonstrates how a preacher can get in touch with God's Word in Scripture both through sensing the human situation between the lines of the passage and through becoming aware of the life within the form, structure, and tone of those lines. Now let us return to the main question: What sermon forms can help today's hearers so enter into a passage of Scripture that the hearers themselves experience something of the life-changing effects of that pericope? Contextual sermon forms take their lead from the human situation giving rise to the passage as well as from the life moving through the shape and style of the passage. Through a judicious choice of sermon form, for instance, the dynamic of Paul pleading for Philippian unity through a powerful Christological hymn can be brought into the dynamic of a contemporary congregation whose struggle with disunity needs the uniting vision of this Christ hymn.

One sermon form that would embody and release Phil. 2:5–11 could pick up on the human situation giving rise to this passage. The preacher could begin with a scene of bickering Christians in Philippi, followed by a parallel scene in First Steeple Church, Midtown, U.S.A. The sermon flow could then shift to a Roman house, where Paul under guard dictates a letter remembering thankfully his Philippian colleagues in Christ. But Paul goes on to plead for the kind of mind in the Philippian community that could transcend petty differences because it is a mind saturated with the self-emptying Christ. This kind of mind is a way of thinking and feeling about oneself in relation to God that becomes the enabling ground for obedient service. This is the mind of a person who perceives that because of what the hymn describes (2:6–11) he or she now is a person of different orientation toward God, self, and others, and who stands secure with a new capacity to pour self out for others. This mind comes as a gift from Christ, discovered in community ("in Christ Jesus" in 2:5 can be taken as a corporate term as well as an individual term), making possible new capabilities for self-sacrifice as a result of the self-giving experienced in this community. The sermon could picture Paul recalling good times with the Philippians, humming again the hymns they sang together, particularly one that begins, "Though he was in the form of God." Next, the sermon's "eye" could focus on the good times of First Steeple congregation which suffuse the heart with joy, scenes of celebration in times of triumph as well as pictures of mutual support in times of tragedy. Then the preacher might invite the hearers to stare deeply into the cross hanging in the chancel. The self-emptying that such a cross symbolizes signals the emptying which Paul sings about. The community's *kenosis* can turn fragmentation into oneness in Christ. The sermon could close with scenes of unity at First Steeple engendered by this Christly *kenosis*.

Other contextual sermon shapes could take their cues from the shape of the language itself in Phil. 2:5–11. A sermon could be formed by the parabola shape of the hymn itself, beginning with an imagined scene with the Godhead in heaven where ultimate prerogatives of power and authority are exercised and enjoyed. The sermon could then move to Act II where Christ surrenders these prerogatives so that his followers through his death may taste of these ultimate prerogatives in their own humanity, and then to Act III, where God exalts this *kenosis* as sign of the shape of authentic humanity itself. Having set up this a-b-a shape for the hearers, the sermon could then spin out several more parabola-shaped scenes that depict the gospel reality of this kind of humanity, stories actual or imagined that show disunity moving toward unity as a result of the self-emptying life-style of the Christian community.

Another contextual form for a sermon on this passage could begin prosaically with brief arguments for the need for unity among quarreling Christians, arguments interrupted, however, by the "music" of Christ's saving *kenosis*. The sermon could actually shift from prose to paean, with the preacher trying a poetic or lyrical style that pictures the community with the mind of Christ putting an end to separations through obedient crucifixion of petulant self-interest.

Finally, one more sermon shape could allow the congregation to relive the power of contrast found within the language of the

Christ hymn. The sermon's action could move through a series of juxtapositions: form of God/form of servant; holding all/pouring out all; death to all prerogatives (cross)/elevation to true prerogatives (exaltation). Part one could picture self-serving, with contemporaries grabbing at all the gusto they can get in affluence, station, and status, and holding to those "prerogatives" as if holding to breathing itself. Part two contrasts with part one with pictures of the mind of Christ working in people who know how to "let go (true autonomy)," to pour out self—not in some exquisite self-annihilation, but rather in an emptying of self as a discovery of self (exaltation).

Whatever the shape of a contextual sermon on Phil. 2:5–11, however, the preacher will want to offer it with Paul's loving, pastoral tone. The hearers, however divided, cranky, and abrasive, are still "beloved."

Qualities of Contextual Sermons

Two important qualities about contextual sermon shapes need brief attention. First, these shapes major in narrative material, featuring scenes or clusters of scenes of things that happen to human beings. By contrast, the traditional discursive sermon is shaped predominantly in the reflective mode, with narrative or metaphorical parts assigned the old role of illustrations designed to provide an earthly picture for a heavenly idea primarily as a means of relieving the tedium of abstractions. Contextual sermon shapes do not so much banish reflection as they relocate pondering within the flow of narration. In so doing, such sermon shapes model the way the preacher thinks about things amid the flow of life, a fit paradigm for the relationship of reason to revelation. Such shapes avoid the pretension of assuming that action should be solely subordinate to or should stem from reflection (a questionable assumption of the Enlightenment[19]). Further, the contextual sermon form, in setting up pauses for reflection amid the flow of narration, resists the more recent temptation to baptize narrative itself as sufficient vehicle for the Word in Scripture without some attendant reflection. While some preachers show sufficient skill with narrative sermons to need little or no reflective passages to aid the sermon's impact, many other preachers who attempt narrative-only sermons too often leave their hearers stranded in the story line for lack of clarity about the sermon's intent.

A second important attribute of the contextual sermon shape in preaching is that working with these shapes both demands and bolsters an active imagination.[20] This is imagination not in the sense of decorating the plain walls of reason, nor in the sense of juxtaposing words or images to catch the eye. Rather, this is imagination that bridges intelligence and experience, opening the way for a full engagement with life. Imagination through narratives, metaphors, and images constantly relocates ideas along experiential lines until those ideas evolve or break into insight. Imagination enables the preacher to sense how people feel, to know their symbolic and prerational life. Imagination places at the preacher's fingertips clusters of symbols and metaphors that galvanize human motivation. With cultivated imagination the preacher looks both between the lines and deep into the language to sense the reality of that passage. From such a creative stance the preacher combines basic investigative work on authorship, setting, and structure of the scriptural text with the intuitive, venturesome, and spontaneous exercise of seeing in the mind's eye the life of the text meeting the life of the congregation. Imagination serves as the preacher's catalyst for melding contexts. In Amos Wilder's words, "Imagination is a necessary component of all profound knowing and celebration; all remembering, realizing and anticipating; all faith, hope and love."[21]

The Text / ACTS 10:9–29
EXEGETICAL OBSERVATIONS

Acts 10:9–29 can be understood only in the larger context of Acts 10:1 to 11:18. In the tenth chapter Luke presents the story of how God directly intervenes with Cornelius and Peter to bring about a baptism of the Holy Spirit upon the Gentiles. In 11:1–18 Peter defends his actions before his Jewish Christian colleagues in Jerusalem.

The model previously used lifts up for comment three important components that belong to the formation of this block of material: the question raised, the author's intent, and the hearers' mind-set.[22] With Acts 10:1 to 11:18 Luke joins a key struggle in the primitive church regarding whether or not the observance of Jewish law is obligatory for all Christians. The Judaizing party of the Christian church was insisting that all Gentile converts be circumcised and submit to the law. This tenth chapter questions that mind-set with the dramatic account of the dream (10:9–16) which convinces Peter (10:28) that he should discriminate against no one in presenting the gospel. God leads Peter to share this insight with the Roman centurion Cornelius and his household (10:1–8, 17–48). While Peter preaches to Cornelius' household the gospel in terms of God's impartiality (10:34ff.), the Holy Spirit falls on those Gentiles who believe (10:44). Peter marks this Gentile Pentecost by ordering those who received the Holy Spirit to be baptized with water.

Luke exercises several intentions in using these materials. First, to the Jewish Christians he announces that God has taken a special initiative to communicate to the church that Gentile converts are not expected to adhere to the law. Secondly, to all Christians, Luke presents a picture of Peter's leadership that keeps a healthy balance between Jewish and Gentile factions in the church. Thirdly, to both the Jewish and the Roman authorities Luke insists that the rise of Christianity is God's business and not just an undertaking of mortals (see Acts 5:38f.). Here Luke responds to a mind-set promoted by Jews in power, that the Christian movement is counterfeit, worthy only to be stamped out by Rome as a subversive movement. Luke strives with these materials, therefore, for more toleration of the church by the Roman state.

The language and design of the passage suggest that the narrative form of the pericope lends itself naturally to a narrativelike sermon on this passage. Further, repetitive structure of the materials becomes a message in itself of how God radically intervened to effect the "Gentile Pentecost" (10:3, 13, 19). Luke repeatedly has his characters recall how God comes *directly* to them in God's concern to communicate that God shows no partiality in the kingdom (10:28, 30; 11:7, 12). In effect, Luke uses the structure of this passage to emphasize that impartiality in the spreading of the gospel is God's urgent, pointed concern.

With the tone of the passage Luke highlights the drama and wonder inherent in the event itself. The Lucan eye for excitement, color, and action works effectively here, developing in the reader the sense of awe necessary to experience God's invading presence in this event (10:4, 17, 25, 45, 46). The breathtaking moments in this narrative accentuate all the more God's insistence that there be no second-class citizens in the church.

Finally, several images in the passage need particular comment. Three times (10:14, 28; 11:8) Luke has Peter using the term "unclean," a metaphor for "alien" or "undesirable." While "unclean" was used for centuries by Jews as a cultic term related to ritualistic propriety, the expression also took on a social dimension by serving as a metaphor for such acts as fornication, idolatry, and similar unethical actions.[23] The ritual purity maintained for centuries at the heart of Israel's life in the temple cult apparently symbolized the Jews' broader concern to protect themselves from social contamination that would weaken their identity as a people. In this passage the term "unclean" obviously serves as a metaphor for "non-Jewish," "common," or "alien." To become unclean as a first-century Jew, then, was to be cast with those who did not share Jewish mores and ethical values. This notion of social impurity, however effective a means of social control by Jewish priests and hierarchy, virtually paralyzed any missionary efforts by Jewish Christians in Luke's day. Jewish Christians allowed themselves contact with Gentiles only when Gentiles assumed Jewish manners and mores. Luke combats this exclusivism and its underlying fear through the agency of the dream that pictures Christ himself demanding that Peter cease making such artificial distinctions between the "pure" and the "impure." This first-century issue translates today into a similar issue involving the majority of mainline Christians who fear reaching out to those whose values, mores, and life-style are different. The sermon will picture those church folk in middle-class, mainline America who feel squeamish about "touching the unclean." The sermon challenges the hearers in the name of Christian mission to transcend distinctions of taste and temperament. Even more important, the sermon finishes by offering the succor at Christ's table necessary for encouraging Christians to reach out.

Images of food and table also play an important role in the passage. Peter dreams of unclean animals at the dinner hour (10:9) when hungry (10:10) and surrounded by "unclean" animal hides (9:43). In the dream he strives with Christ over eating unclean meat (10:12–16). Gentiles spend the night with Peter and thus, by implication, spend time with him at table (10:23). In his sermon to the Gentiles, Peter reminds his hearers that the risen Christ was made manifest to his disciples in the context of their eating and drinking with him (10:41). Finally, Peter seals the coming of the Holy Spirit upon the Gentiles by spending some days with them afterward (10:48), again implying time at table with them. Further, the Judaizers challenge Peter in terms of his eating with the Gentiles (11:3), while Peter recounts his dream in terms of the issue of eating common meat (11:7–8). The table as the locus of acceptance and intimacy, therefore, figures in both the text and the sermon as a central metaphor that holds up both the issue of exclusivism in the church and the possibility of our acceptance as "clean" in Jesus Christ.

A third image, the seaport of Joppa, serves as an important symbol of the avoidance of mission to the Gentiles. Just as Jonah tried to escape God's call to mission from Joppa (Jonah 1:3), so at Joppa, Peter wrestles with that same impulse to evade mission in his dream. Assuming that the cloth (Acts 10:11) holding the animals in the dream is a sailcloth from a ship, we feel a profound tension in the use of the word in the dream. The very cloth that would be a ship's sail carrying Peter away from Joppa and his missional calling becomes the vehicle for confronting Peter with that responsibility in Joppa. Joppa becomes in the sermon, then, the refuge of exclusivists where God comes to jar the church loose from fear-filled partiality.

The narrative structure of the passage lends itself naturally to a sermon along narrative lines. The sermon moves on these story lines to expose the issues of exclusivism and the tendency of most

Christians out of fear to allow distinctions of values and life-style to become barriers between them and those to whom they are called to offer Jesus Christ. Further, the sermon tries to approximate in dramatic form God's direct, confrontive intervention into human consciousness, pushing the hearer in grace to make way for all who would come to Christ's table.

Sermon / INVITING OTHERS TO OUR TABLE

The scene: the bustling Gentile seaport of Joppa. Peter sits on the rooftop porch of Simon the tanner. It is noon, and he stares at the tall sails of fishing boats nearby. He tries to pray, as is his noonday custom, but he is restless and preoccupied. The smell of cooking food downstairs reminds him of his hunger.

Through reflection couched in narration I now establish a polarity between Peter's scrupulosity and Simon the tanner's uncleanness.

But the other smell, of those freshly tanned animal hides drying in the sun, tells him that he is surrounded by uncleanness. When he goes downstairs to eat, he, the scrupulous Jewish Christian, will go down to an unclean table and the sight of his host, Simon the tanner. Simon will eat with hands permanently stained with tanning acid. And behind Simon, those animal hides will hang there, beasts Peter would hardly touch, much less eat.

Peter puts back his head and closes his eyes. He wonders why the Lord wants him in Joppa anyway. Here he is surrounded by all this Gentile uncleanness, trying to start a new colony of Christians. But the unclean table these days revives the old revulsion of Gentiles that he learned long ago at a separate, clean table when he was a child.

I identify Peter with Jonah by using Joppa as a symbol of the avoidance of mission (Jonah 9:3).

He wonders: "Why should I have to bother with these common people in spreading the gospel? Better to be like Jonah, who

caught a ship here in Joppa to escape a mission to the Gentiles,
than to have to offer Christ to these *others.*" The noontide heat
intensifies; Peter slips into a dream.

Peter can't believe what he sees. Coming down from the sky,
wrapped in a huge sailcloth, a great bundle of all kinds of beasts,
reptiles, and fowl. And the voice of Christ: "Rise, kill, eat!" But
Peter's soul is too tied to that childhood table. "No, Lord; for I
have never eaten anything common or unclean." Christ answers,
"What God has cleansed, you must not call common."

*I heighten the conflict between the living Christ and Peter with
dramatic dialogue.*

Again, the insistent Christ: "Rise, kill, eat!" Again the stubborn,
prejudiced Peter: "No, no, no, Lord, I can't eat that kind of meat!"
Again, Christ answers, "What God has cleansed, you must not call
common." A third time the demanding Christ: "Rise, kill, eat!"
Now, fully frustrated, Peter cries, "No, no, no, Lord, I can't do it,
I can't do it!" Echoes of other threefold litanies with Christ, such
as, "Peter, I go to Jerusalem to die." "NO, NO, NO, LORD!"
"Peter, this night you will deny me three times," "NO, NO, NO,
LORD!" And now, "Peter, rise, kill, eat! Rise, kill, eat!" "NO, NO,
NO, LORD!"

*Now comes interpretive, reflective work within the flow of
narrative.*

The cries seem the last wretched convulsion of the demon of
prejudice that has to come out. The denials seem to drive the
strange, flying menagerie back up into the sky to end the dream

But what a difference between the rebellious Peter in the dream
and the cooperative Peter after the dream. The same Peter who
shouts, "NO, NO, NO," in the dream becomes genial host to
Cornelius' servants, and probably sat down to eat with them. The
same Peter who railed at Christ in the dream hikes thirty miles the
next day to admit to Cornelius that he will never call anyone
common or unclean again. This same Peter readily baptizes Cornelius and his people and is content to stay there some days,

probably sitting down to eat with them. Those whom God cleansed Peter no longer calls common.

I complete this section with reflective work flowing out of the narrative.

How do we explain the difference? The resistance in the dream seems the final frenzy of the powers of death as they loosen their grip on Peter's prejudice. The NO, NO, NO! sounds like the birth pangs of a new openness. Peter did some heavy and necessary work in his dreams.

Another scene: the bustling Joppa of your life, with its commerce of frustrations, false barriers, and dreams.

Joppa is now translated into a symbol of our bustling, restless life. I identify the hearers with Peter.

You, a latter-day Simon Peter, in your noontide heat of restlessness and preoccupation. You keep finding yourself at table with people who seem unclean. In Joppa it's not like it used to be. People don't look like they ought to look in Joppa.

I make a cultural translation of uncleanness in Joppa. I dramatize disdain by contemporary Peter for the contemporary "Gentiles."

They don't wear Jordache jeans and Gant shirts like they ought to. Instead, they make the scene in yellow tank shirts and purple socks. Some wear grossly upswept hair, and wobble by on long, thin spiked heels. Some don't care if their hair is swept up or down. It's frizzy, unwashed, unparted . . . ungodly. They're unclean nowadays in Joppa.

They don't act like they ought to act here in Joppa. They're not smooth enough for our table. They snort when they laugh at parties. They talk too loud, swig their beer, belch in front of their neighbors. Some give a red-neck "10-4, good buddy" on their two-way radios, a sound not too pleasant in Joppa.

Some in Joppa are unsettled sexually. Some are having babies without husbands, and choose to raise them alone in spite of our frowns. Some have come out of their closet to say they are gay and we in Joppa don't know what to say. Some say sex belongs more to a relationship than to the institution of marriage, and we don't know how to respond with much that makes sense . . . here in Joppa.

They're so unclean here in Joppa. They don't value what's important to us. Some don't value work the way we do in Joppa. Some don't want to get ahead, and even want us to tell them where "ahead" is when we get there. Some don't want our 7:18 train in the morning, and don't care for the 5:18 evening express either. They're not awed by our steeple or by our pastor, nor are they moved by the organ and the stained glass. They're not even sure what sin is anymore. They live together without commitment and then sue for palimony. It's so unclean here nowadays in Joppa.

I pick up here on Peter's desire to escape God's call to him to minister to the Gentiles.

O to hop ship and clear out of Joppa! To leave those aliens who should have been Anglos. To leave those crude folk for the smooth folk. To leave those unstable people for together people. And to cry with Peter, "Why should I have to bother with these people, Lord?"

I introduce the underlying fear that fuels the anger expressed above, to begin exposing the root of the problem.

Yes, Peter, we can hear the anger in your voice. But even more, we can sense the fear that underlies it all.

The noonday heat intensifies, and you, Peter, slip into a dream. Out of the sky comes a great picnic cloth holding a weird assortment of 150 people.

This assortment represents the "Gentiles" we middle class feel uncomfortable with.

You see whiners, demanders, seducers, cheaters. You see blacks, yellows, browns, reds, whites. You see the supercool and the very uptight. You see experimental dudes and revolutionary cats.

I now revisit the conflict in the earlier dramatic dialogue.

Then, the voice says, "Set your table for these." You respond, "No, Lord, I don't eat with these." But Christ rejoins: "What God has cleansed, you must not call common. Set your table for these!" Now you're stubborn: "No, no, Lord, I can't get with these." "What God has cleansed, you must not call common," Christ keeps insisting. A third time the demand, "Set your table for these." Now you're boiling: "NO! NO! NO! LORD, I CAN'T, I CAN'T."

Now comes interpretive work through this same dialogue form within the flow of the narrative.

The last convulsion of a defeated demon: "I can't change the fact that mainline Christianity seems to be for the privileged only; I can't change the fact that most of us go to church to get rather than to give; I can't change the fact that most of us work with an antiseptic Christianity that is attracted only to the clean; I can't change the fact that many of us are so preoccupied with bazaars, banquets, and Bible study that we have little time to worry about refugee families, suicide centers, drug abuse, and unfair employment; I can't change the fact that those unclean ones don't seem to care, don't want to be decent. Lord, these unclean don't deserve our effort!" Listen to you, Peter. That fear is boiling up out of you. You're doing some heavy and necessary work in your dreams.

And look again, Peter. Your heavy dreamwork seems to be paying off. How else do we explain the difference between your resistant self in the dream and your cooperative self after the dream?

I now describe ways grace works in the aftermath of contemporary dreamwork.

This same you who shouts, "NO! NO! NO!" in the dream, who shouted "NO" in 1964 with the civil rights legislation, who shouted "NO" in 1968 when your child marched on the Pentagon, now finds yourself at the bargaining table on Tuesday with people you once swore you'd never talk to. This same you we see on Wednesday night at Village Hall with types you turned your back on five years ago. This same you we see at the breakfast table this morning with your daughter's husband whom you once said you'd never speak to again. This same you who rails at Christ in the dream goes thirty miles out of the way to say to a woman that you apologize for your sexist jokes, that you are not only unsure about what to do with her sexuality, but also you are not that certain about what to do with your own. This same you that habitually fences off your table, now finds yourself no longer that comfortable only with Norman Rockwell faces around the table. What God has cleansed, Peter, you are no longer content to call common!

What's going on in you, Peter? You're breaking bread with a different breed of people today. What God has cleansed, you no longer call common. Something has come out of you, kicking and screaming. You seem more at ease now.

I move finally to the root issue, the hearers' sense of uncleanness.

It didn't come easily, did it, Peter? It rarely does come easily, such basic change. You always did resent those unclean folk, mainly because you never felt you were that clean. At bottom the real issue has been *your* uncleanness, hasn't it, Peter? How much easier to see others' shortcomings than your own! That's the way it is with all of us.

But then the Christ who pushed you in your dream kept setting his own table with a name place for you, Peter. Frequently, he kept inviting you to his bread and cup. He knows all about you, Peter, your wiles, your betrayal, your fear, your uncleanness. Even so he wants you at his table, Peter. And then he speaks: "What God has cleansed, you must not call common." Peter, he's talking about you! He's insisting you are clean.

No wonder, Peter, your table is beginning to look more and more like his.

NOTES

1. Goethe, *Faust,* tr. C. F. MacIntyre (New Directions, 1949), p. 37.

2. For a helpful discussion in this regard, see Brevard S. Childs, *Introduction to the Old Testament as Scripture* (Fortress Press, 1979). D. Moody Smith, in his *Interpreting the Gospels for Preaching* (Fortress Press, 1980), writes to show preachers how to employ form and redaction criticism in building sermons. Three other volumes that are basic for interpretation are: Martin Dibelius, *A Fresh Approach to the New Testament and Early Christian Literature* (Charles Scribner's Sons, 1936); Rudolf Bultmann, *The History of the Synoptic Tradition* (Harper & Row, 1963); Klaus Kloch, *The Growth of the Biblical Tradition,* tr. S. M. Cupitt (Charles Scribner's Sons, 1969).

3. Elizabeth Achtemeier, "The Artful Dialogue," *Interpretation,* Vol. 35, No. 1 (Jan. 1981), p. 26.

4. James A. Sanders, "The Bible as Canon," *The Christian Century,* Dec. 2, 1981, p. 1251.

5. Here I use the word "significant," in the same way that Eric D. Hirsch, Jr., uses it in his *Validity in Interpretation* (Yale University Press, 1967). Hirsch distinguishes between the meaning of a passage and its importance or *significance* for its readers/hearers.

6. Richard E. Palmer, in his *Hermeneutics* (Northwestern University Press, 1969), speaks of the art of listening for the question that presumes the passage: "To understand a text . . . is to understand the question behind the text, the question that called the text into being. Literary interpretation . . . needs to develop an openness for creative negativity, for learning something it could not anticipate or foresee" (p. 250).

7. Paul Ricoeur, *Interpretation Theory* (Texas Christian University Press, 1976), p. 92.

8. Jay Schleusener, "Convention and the Context of Reading," and John C. Sherwood, "Prolegomena to Any Future Criticism Which Shall Make Sense," *Critical Inquiry,* Vol. 6, No. 4 (Summer 1980), pp. 669–690.

9. Schleusener, loc. cit., p. 680.

10. Sherwood, loc. cit., p. 684. For more on the hermeneutical experience as intrinsically historical, see Palmer, *Hermeneutics,* pp. 242–253. See also Michael Polanyi, *Personal Knowledge* (London: Routledge & Kegan Paul, 1958).

11. For particular assistance on the hymnic form, see the following by Ralph P. Martin: *An Early Christian Confession* (London: Tyndale Press, 1960); *Worship in the Early Church* (Wm. B. Eerdmans Publishing Co., 1964), pp. 39–52; "The Form-analysis of Philippians ii, 5–11," in *Studia Evangelica,* II/III, ed. F. L. Cross (Berlin: Akademie-Verlag, 1964), pp. 611–620.

12. Amos Wilder, *Theopoetic* (Fortress Press, 1976), p. 2.

13. Note Richard L. Rohrbach, *The Biblical Interpreter* (Fortress Press, 1978); Bernard B. Scott, *Jesus, Symbol Maker for the Kingdom* (Fortress Press, 1981).

14. A spate of literature in recent years trumpets self-interest as the key to self-fulfillment. See Robert J. Ringer, *Looking Out for Number One* (Funk & Wagnalls, 1977).

15. For a good introduction to the impact of form on readers/hearers, see William A. Beardslee, *Literary Criticism of the New Testament* (Fortress Press, 1970). For entrée to structural criticism of Scripture, see Edgar V. McKnight, *Meaning in Texts* (Fortress Press, 1978); Daniel Patte, *What Is Structural Exegesis?* ed. Dan O. Via, Jr. (Fortress Press, 1976). For the literary stance, see Robert Detweiler, *Story, Sign, and Self,* ed. William A. Beardslee (Fortress Press, 1978).

16. Martin, *Worship in the Early Church,* pp. 49f.

17. David G. Buttrick, "Interpretation and Preaching," *Interpretation,* Vol. 35, No. 1 (Jan. 1981), p. 50.

18. We follow here the principle of polarity which William D. Thompson stresses in our sharpening the meaning of the text. "Text and Sermon," *Interpretation,* Vol. 35, No. 1 (Jan. 1981), p. 26.

19. For a good discussion of key flaws in exegesis that leans on the presuppositions of the Enlightenment, see Hans W. Frei, *The Eclipse of the Biblical Narrative* (Yale University Press, 1974).

20. Robert D. Young, *Religious Imagination: God's Gift to Prophets and Preachers* (Westminster Press, 1979), focuses specifically on the relationship between imagination and preaching. See also Richard A. Jensen, *Telling the Story: Variety and Imagination in Preaching* (Augsburg Publishing House, 1980); James A. Sanders, *God Has a Story Too* (Fortress Press, 1979); Edmund A. Steimle, Morris J. Niedenthal, and Charles L. Rice, *Preaching the Story* (Fortress Press, 1980).

21. Wilder, *Theopoetic,* p. 2.

22. For incisive assistance in interpreting Acts, see F. F. Bruce, *Commentary on The Book of The Acts* (Wm. B. Eerdmans Publishing Co., 1954); Henry J. Cadbury, *The Making of Luke-Acts* (London: S.P.C.K.,

1958); Hans Conzelmann, *The Theology of St. Luke* (Harper & Brothers, 1960); Ernst Haenchen, *The Acts of the Apostles, A Commentary* (Westminster Press, 1971); Leander Keck and J. Louis Martyn, *Studies in Luke-Acts* (Abingdon Press, 1966), particularly pp. 258–278; William Neil, *The Acts of the Apostles* (London: Oliphants, 1973).

23. For a fascinating discussion of the evolution of the term, and of the idea of purity in ancient Judaism, see Jacob Neusner, *The Idea of Purity in Ancient Judaism* (Leiden: E. J. Brill, 1973).

3

Shaping Sermons by Plotting the Text's Claim Upon Us

Thomas G. Long

FORMING THE SERMON

The Lively Encounter: Sermon Form and Content

Reduced to the simplest of terms, the development of a sermon involves two principal activities: the marshaling of material (biblical exegesis, illustrations, quotations, etc.) and the arranging of that material into a coherent pattern, shape, or structure. The second of these two activities, the task of forming, organizing, and structuring sermons, has rarely been considered one of the livelier, more creative dimensions of preaching. Victimized by tedious classroom exercises in "sermon outlining," most preachers can be forgiven if they find the job of structuring a sermon to be not only dull but also peripheral, standing at some distance from the more central issues of biblical interpretation and the development of communicative content.

Some of the older homiletical literature unfortunately did much to reinforce the idea that a sermon's design could be constructed as an afterthought. The prevailing notion was that a preacher possessed an arsenal of sermon structure options (often designated by catchy labels such as "The Jewel" or "The Ladder") into which the content of almost any sermon could be poured, like gelatin into a mold. There was encouragement, of course, somehow to match the sermon content to the most amenable prefabricated shape, but this could never quite hide the fact that content and design were developed independently and according to differing criteria: biblical-theological vs. rhetorical.

Properly understood, however, the task of organizing and structuring a sermon is not peripheral at all; it is central and vital to the impact of the sermon. In our understanding of *communication* as the sharing of meaning which shapes personal and corporate identity, a sermon structure becomes a communication strategy, a plan for enabling the sermon to have meaning. This is not merely to repeat the conventional wisdom that how one says something communicates as effectively as what one says. Rather, it is to claim that content and structure in a sermon *combine* to produce a communication effect greater than their sum. There is, for good or ill, a lively interaction between form and content to the point that it becomes no longer meaningful to speak of "form" and "content" as independent realities; rather, the whole sermon can be considered as "the form of the content."

Achieving this sort of unity between form and content involves a fundamental shift in the way we understand a sermon. Sermons have often been described in metaphors borrowed from the courtroom or the debate hall. Viewed from this perspective, sermons are legal briefs, or formal arguments, presenting evidence in a persuasive or logical fashion and hoping for a favorable verdict. Whatever value this image of preaching may possess, it is, theologically and functionally speaking, far too narrow. Although the lawyer/debater picture of preaching does not completely exclude the experimental dimension of preaching, it does tend to focus upon the sermon as a conveyor of concepts, concepts that are interrelated according to the principles of formal logic. Preaching becomes a cognitive, intellectual, ideational event. Illustrations become "windows on the word," devices for making concepts plain, with the desired result of preaching to enable the hearers to "remember the points."

Other metaphors used to describe the task of organizing sermons are imported from the field of architecture. Sermon blueprints are drawn. Blocks of material are quarried from biblical commentaries, plays, novels, pastoral experiences, and other resources. They are hewn and chiseled to the correct proportions and fit together to produce a structure which, if successful, is not only strong and functional but also beautiful.

But like images taken from the courtroom, architectural images ultimately prove too limiting. To think of a sermon in architectural terms alone obscures an important dimension of preaching, namely, the temporal dimension. A building, when finished, occurs "all at once"; a sermon takes place over time. In sermons, meaning is not simply asserted; it is developed. It occurs not merely in space, but through time. To be sure, it is possible to experience a building as a temporal journey. Indeed, some architectural masterpieces are designed to be discovered as a series of progressive epiphanies. Such artistic use of the temporal dimension is not fundamental, however, to the architect's craft. It *is* essential to the preacher's craft. Sermons and temples may share many things in common—beauty, symbolism—but they are markedly different in structural conception. The temple must be structurally static or it will fall. The sermon must be structurally fluid or it will perish.

Since sermons have purposes broader and deeper than those of legal arguments, involve patterns of development which are often more intuitional than scholastically logical and more emotional than cognitional, and involve not only the organization of content but also the organization of time, other images and metaphors are needed to illumine the task of creating sermons.

Between "Tick" and "Tock": Sermonic Stress

Literary critic Frank Kermode has suggested the metronomic rhythm of a clock as one basic image of structured time and, consequently, as a metaphor for the structuring of time which takes place in a literary creation:

> Let us take a very simple example, the ticking of a clock. . . . *Tick* is our word for a physical beginning, *tock* is our word for an end. We say they differ. What enables them to be different is a special kind of middle. We can perceive a duration only when it is organized. . . . The clock's *tick-tock* I take to be a model of what we call a plot, an organization that humanizes time by giving it form.[1]

The interval between *tick* and *tock* is not "dead silence." It is a special time, alive time, able to be weighed, measured, and felt, because it is *organized* time. The raw, undisciplined substance of time is shaped by the brackets *tick* and *tock*. The time between *tick* and *tock* does not merely pass; it is plotted. Moreover, if Kermode is correct that a plot is "an organization that humanizes time by giving it form," then sermons can be said to be plotted, too.[2] Sermons "humanize time" in the deepest theological sense of "humanize." Sermons are expressions of what happens when the gospel shapes time and, thus, redeems the time.

This points toward a new and controlling metaphor for the task of forming a sermon. The one who shapes a sermon is not a lawyer, a debater, or an architect, but rather a *creator of plots.* It is tempting to slip, at this point, into the more prevalent language of the day and to claim that what we mean is that the preacher is a "storyteller." This is partly true, and the designation "storyteller" is surely more suggestive and congenial than the less vibrant term "creator of plots." Yet to exchange the terms would be misleading. Sermons cannot always be stories; they sometimes do not even include stories, but they must always have *plots,* patterns of dynamic, sequential elements.[3] In this sense, the sermon is storylike, even when it includes no stories per se. Stories can simply be told; plots must be planned. Plots are the routes of journeys between tick and tock.

It would be easy enough to say that the tick of a sermon is its *introduction* and the tock its *conclusion.* While this may, in a sense, be true, it imposes older, more static categories upon the notion of sermon "plots." Sermon introductions are often thought of as formal devices for presenting in miniature the whole theme of a sermon. Conclusions are, of course, their mirror images providing final summaries of the sermon substance. According to traditional homiletical wisdom, neither introductions nor conclusions should be very long, lest they overshadow the body—the "meat"—of the sermon, and together they should provide balance, a kind of symmetry, for the sermon as a totality.

The tick and the tock of a literary plot do not, however, provide symmetry; they are not mirror-imaged equals. Tick anticipates tock and moves toward it. A literary plot gives meaning to form not merely by arranging it into an interesting and balanced pattern, but rather by applying a kind of *end stress* which energizes the plot development toward a *denouement,* which maintains, in Kermode's words

> within that interval following *tick* a lively expectation of *tock,* and a sense that however remote *tock* may be, all that happens happens as if *tock* were certainly following. As such, plotting presupposes and requires that *an end will bestow upon the whole duration and meaning.*[4]

It is the tock, the denouement, of a sermon that governs, shapes, and gives meaning to the tick, the beginning of the sermon, and to the interval that lies between. Sermons that are plotted are not formed from the beginning to the end, but rather from the end to the beginning. This does not mean, of course, that sermons are somehow written "backward," but rather that even as a sermon is begun the preacher apprehends the ending. Everything in a plot strains forward, anticipating the end, working toward its consummation. Sermons are not propelled by powerful beginnings; they are evoked by significant endings. Or, perhaps better, powerful beginnings are summoned by significant endings. Sermons are not characterized by the unfolding of that which is already apparent, but by the anticipation of that which will be. Sermons are thus, in a sense, literary parallels to their progenitor, the "gospel" genre itself, a literary form in which virtually every element of plot is shaped by its denouement, the passion.

The Shaping of Sermon Plots: Practice

How, then, does one go about the business of "plotting" a sermon? Rules for this process are neither feasible nor desirable, since the shape of a given sermon will be governed by the variables peculiar to a particular preaching occasion. Beyond this, plot formulas (e.g., problem—complication—resolution) should be resisted as literary clichés and as abuses of the creativity of both preacher and hearer. Some general guidelines can be stated, however, which can assist in the structuring of sermons:

1. The place to begin, as we have seen, is with the tock, the ending, the denouement of the sermon. The source of this ending

is the biblical text upon which the sermon is based. Rather than venturing into hermeneutical issues beyond our present scope, I will simply observe that biblical texts are not inert: they interact with each new situation brought to them. To say that biblical texts become Word of God for our situation is to say that biblical texts make ultimate claims upon us. They "intend" certain meanings, meanings that demand responses of faith and action from those who hear them. The end of biblical *interpretation* is to discover an ancient text's claim upon our new situation. As Leander Keck has put it, "There is an intuitive, imaginative, venturesome, spontaneous quality to all interpretation."[5] The end of preaching is to express that textual claim, to allow the text to make its demand and invite response from the contemporary hearers. A sermon cannot begin with this claim; we are not ready to hear it. A sermon must end, however, with this claim, and no other. The claim of this text for these people at this moment is the end of preaching and the denouement of this sermon.

2. Once the preacher/interpreter has done all that can be done to discover the claim of a biblical text and positioned that claim as the outcome of the sermon, the sermon itself is governed by that ending and becomes a process for allowing that claim to be heard, felt, and responded to. This works to make the sermon both complete and economical, since all that is necessary for the hearing of the textual claim needs to be included, but all that is extraneous to that claim can be pared away.

Hearing the claim of a text is, of course, a complex process, often involving *cognitive* elements (things we need to know: e.g., the fact that Jesus ate with sinners, Paul's relationship to the Galatian churches, or the meaning of the word "slave"), *emotional* elements (feelings we need to experience: e.g., joy, penitence, or acceptance), *behavioral* elements (actions we are called upon to perform: e.g., praising God, serving neighbor, or forgiving those who have wronged us).

The "plotting" of a sermon involves (1) deciding which of these elements is necessary for the hearing of a claim and (2) arranging those elements in a sequence that anticipates the claim and is most conducive to enabling a response to the claim. Suppose the sermon hopes to enable the claim of Paul's words to the Philippians to come alive: "Rejoice in the Lord always" (Phil. 4:4). Do the hearers need to *know* some things (e.g., the theological meaning of the words "rejoice in the Lord") before they can *do* this kind of rejoicing, or do they perhaps need to *feel* the emotion of joy in an "ordinary" way before they can comprehend the theological depths of "rejoicing in the Lord"? There are, of course, no set answers to questions like these. Answers must be given out of the preacher's own awareness of each specific preaching situation, but, once formulated, they govern the way the components of the sermon are arranged.

Often the biblical text itself can provide a pattern for shaping the sermon, since texts are themselves fashioned in such a way as to make their claims heard. Sermons on the parable of the Good Samaritan, for example, often spend most of their time asserting the text's claim "Go and do likewise," pointing out our failure to act as neighbor and areas of need where we can show the kind of compassion evidenced by the Samaritan. All of this is unmindful of the part that the text does not *begin* with this claim, but ends with it, inserting it only after the parabolic process has taken place. If recent critics are correct, the parable invites hearers to identify with the traveler who is thrown into the ditch—in a sense, to "become" this character in the parable. Thus, the call to "go and do likewise" comes only *after* the experience of being cared for, "neighbored," in a gracious and unexpected way. A sermon on this parable might do well to follow the wisdom of the parable's own plot structure and to provide moments for the congregation to experience or to reflect upon experiences of grace in their own lives before—and in preparation for—hearing the demand, "Go and do likewise."

In summary, then, the process of "plotting" a sermon involves interpreting a biblical text, allowing its claim upon us to form the aim—or denouement—of the sermon; ascertaining the cognitive, emotional, and behavioral issues that need to be heard (these become, in effect, the *elements* of the sermon plot); and arranging those elements according to the preacher's sense of their communicational connection into a sequence that anticipates and progresses toward the denouement. A schematic of a sermon plot would appear as follows:

Element #1 → Element #2 → Element #3 → Denouement

We are now in a position to explore in more detail how the shaping of one sermon plot might occur, beginning with the exegesis of the text and moving through to the full sermon.

The Text / MARK 11:11–25
EXEGETICAL OBSERVATIONS

Mark 11:11–25 is composed of three main sections: the cursing of the fig tree (11:11–14), the cleansing of the Temple (11:15–19), and the teachings on faith and prayer (11:20–25).

Because of the obvious difficulties with the incident of the fig tree, commentators have not provided much help for one who wishes to preach on this passage. The depiction of Jesus cursing a fig tree because it did not bear fruit out of season has been called "inherently irrational,"[6] "frankly incredible,"[7] and in "conflict with Jesus' character."[8]

Sometimes an attempt to redeem the text has been made by allowing the fig tree curse to stand as a "parable in action" of God's displeasure over the barrenness of Judaism. On the positive side, the "solution" to the dilemma of the text does connect the fig tree incident to the subsequent account of the cleansing of the Temple. It finally proves to be at best a partial, and thus unsatisfactory, rendering of the text's meaning, however, because it does not deal with the principal offense of the text: Jesus' expectation of fruit from the tree *out of season*. The notion of a barren, and thus guilty, Israel may work to explain the Matthean account of this incident (Matt. 21:18–19), where the out-of-season notation is omitted, but it cannot encompass the full meaning of the Marcan text. Something more complex is at play in Mark.

In order to understand the impact of Mark's treatment of this incident, we need to look not so much behind the text to some historical event or legend that could have prompted the text, but rather to the way Mark weaves this passage into the whole fabric of his Gospel. When we grasp the three incidents of the passage as one integrated literary and theological unit, we see that Mark himself provides the key to the understanding of the fig tree incident and the Temple cleansing in the exchange between Peter and Jesus in Mark 11:20–25. Peter points out that the fig tree which Jesus had earlier cursed had withered. The seemingly disconnected response of Jesus on faith and prayer in fact interprets the fig tree event. Using typical Semitic hyperbole, Jesus announces that the withering of the fig tree is connected to the kingdom power of faith and prayer. The fig tree incident points toward the disciples' ability to participate in the kingdom's reversal of the expected order, in the kingdom's bringing in of the *impossible,* like mountains into the sea or figs out of season.

The whole text, then, develops a progressive impact upon the reader. The typical reader of Mark, upon encountering the story of the cursing of the fig tree, will predictably stumble over the line "for it was not the season for figs." (Stumbling over this line is not a product merely of twentieth-century sensitivity. Matthew, as we have noted, stumbles too, thus omitting the line.) Mark *wants* the reader to stumble, invites the reader to exclaim, "But that's impossible, you can't expect fruit out of season." That response anticipates the text's own denouement: "Yes, that's right, that's impossible. Have faith in God's kingdom, and you also will participate in the 'impossible,' casting mountains into the sea and discovering the power of prayer."

Viewed from this perspective, the fig tree story becomes an echo and an additional expression of the saying of Jesus which forms a part of the picture to the entire Jerusalem entry-passion sequence in Mark: "With men it is impossible, but not with God; for all things are possible with God" (Mark 10:27).

The text then exposes the central clash of Mark's Gospel: the old order vs. the new, the powers-that-be vs. the kingdom, the limits of human (and natural) possibility vs. the unlimited divine possibilities, the ordinary season of history vs. the evergreen season of the kingdom.

The Temple officials are denounced by Jesus, then, not merely for barrenness, but for being unresponsive to the breaking in of the "new season": "The time is *now*. The kingdom is at hand." (Mark 1:15). From the perspective of ordinary expectations and the political and religious realities of the day, there is no reason to expect the Temple to embody Isaiah's vision of "a house of prayer for all the nations." Someday, perhaps, but *this* is not the season. That is, not unless, "the time is *now*. The kingdom is at hand."

The claim of this text upon the reader (and therefore the claim that should be embodied in a sermon on this text) is a call to recalibrate expectations. If the Christian community sets expectations according to the ordinary "times and seasons," it will miss signs of the kingdom's power of presence at work in the world. If, however, the community trusts the "new time and season" which has broken into history through Jesus, then it can live its life and do its mission in hope, confident that the work of God is never "out of season."

This text provides, of course, an eschatological hope, not a set of mechanical promises. That is to say, the text is not an invitation to practice magic: Say to *this* mountain, "Be cast into *that* sea," and presto, it will be done. It is, rather, an invitation to practice ministry, calling mountains to be cast into the sea, praying earnestly for God's will to be done, confident that ultimately God will establish his kingdom in fullness and "every valley shall be lifted up, and every mountain and hill be made low."

The literary structure of the total passage gives some clues as to the possible plotting of the sermon. The denouement of the text —the awareness of the new season of the kingdom in which, through God, all things are possible—forms the denouement of the sermon, and the general contours of the text's movement toward that denouement can provide the basic pattern for the development of the sermon:

1. The "offensiveness" of Jesus' action——
    2. The "new season" as expressed in the cleansing of the Temple and as reflected in Mark as a whole——
        3. The expectation and hope of the community living in the "new season": faith, action, prayer. Jesus' "offensive" action seen as gracious sign.

Sermon / FIGS OUT OF SEASON

Well, what do you think about the story of the fig tree?

Jesus and the disciples are on their way from Bethany to Jerusalem when:

> *unfortunately,* Jesus becomes hungry.
>
> *fortunately,* there is nearby the path a fig tree—the kind that produces those fat, succulent, delicious figs in the middle of the summer.
>
> *unfortunately,* it is not the middle of the summer; it is early spring. The little fig tree is doing all it can—it has leaves, but no figs.

What do you expect? It wasn't the season for figs. Evidently Jesus expected something more, because, without so much as a word of explanation, he denounced the fig tree with a withering curse. Within twenty-four hours the little fig tree was *dead.*

Mark 11:11–25 gives the accounts of the cursing of the fig tree, the cleansing of the Temple, and the statements about faith and prayer.

This opening section has three purposes:

1. To indicate, with the opening line, that the hearers' reactions to the story are valued and are integral to the development of the sermon.

2. To provide, in summary form, the essential detail of the first portion of the biblical text.

3. To raise, quite subtly at this point, the question, "What do you expect?" This anticipates the denouement of the sermon.

Now the plot develops . . .

As you can imagine, this story has produced a variety of reactions in people, but in almost all of them there is at least a measure of *shock.*

We seem to have caught Jesus, of all people, in an un-Christlike deed.

This section develops, and permits, the offense of the passage. Communicationally it brings the text into conflict with the hearers' expectations. This conflict of expectations lies at the heart of the text's (and the sermon's) claim and motivates the hearers to "strain forward" toward the resolution—the denouement.

No matter that he was hungry, Jesus, of all people, should have known that a fig tree cannot produce figs out of season.

But no, he *kills* the tree. Albert Schweitzer wouldn't have done that. A member of the Sierra Club wouldn't have done that. Why does Jesus have to do that?

It is some comfort to know that this story has perplexed New Testament scholars and commentators as well. Indeed, a good many of the commentators on Mark treat this story as if *it* were the man in the ditch in the parable of the Good Samaritan and *they* were the priest and the Levite: They pass by silently on the other side! Every now and then one of them pauses long enough to peer into the ditch and be shocked. One commentator, for example, observed: "This is one of the most perplexing stories in the Gospel. . . . What perplexes us is not so much the nature-miracle implied as the unworthy light it casts on the character of Jesus. With our knowledge of Jesus from other sources, we find it frankly incredible that he could have used his power to wither a fig tree because it did not yield figs two or three months before its natural time of fruitage. Let those who will, regard it as a "miracle of judgement"; for ourselves we must ask *Why . . . ?*"[9]

The purpose of this section is to heighten the conflict by providing some scholarly undergirding of the tension.

Why, indeed? Why would the writer of Mark, whose intention is to tell us "the beginning of the good news of Jesus Christ," give us a piece of bad news—a story that reflects unfavorably on the character of Jesus?

Matthew, who follows Mark, tones the story down.

Luke, who follows Mark, won't touch the story with a ten-foot pole. He leaves it out altogether.

One rather psychologically-minded interpreter has suggested that, in this case, maybe the "bad news" is really the "good news." It is difficult to be a follower of a flawless master, and the passage stands as a comforting reminder that even messiahs have their dark days and bad moods. So, the next time we are surly to a waitress, obnoxious with our families, or think withering thoughts about someone at work, we can be comforted by the memory of that day when Jesus got caught with his divinity down and cursed out a little fig tree. Thank goodness it wasn't a disciple —or a Samaritan town!

This section forms, in a sense, a subplot. The material suggests a possible resolution to the conflict previously generated. This section, in which this resolution is rejected as out of accord with the claim of the text, thus highlights the denouement of the text.

We would be tempted to leave it at that—one tiny fleck in the otherwise stainless character of Jesus—were it not for the fact that the writer of Mark practically slaps us in the face with his insistence that this is no playful passage about a peevish Jesus. For he moves immediately to tell us that Jesus went on to Jerusalem, where he engaged in another act of withering violence—throwing the money changers and the buyers and sellers out of the Temple —saying: "Is it not written, 'My house shall be called a house of prayer for all the nations'? But you have made it a den of robbers."

The next day they passed by the fig tree again, and Peter, remembering, cried: "Look, Master! The fig tree you cursed yesterday—it has withered!" Jesus does *not* grin sheepishly, pat Peter on the back and say, "Yeah, I suppose I let things get a little out of hand yesterday."

In this section the subplot which began in the previous section is ended. The psychological "solution" to the conflict is rejected as out of phase with the intention of the text, and . . .

Instead, Jesus says, rather curiously: "Yes . . . have faith in God. Whoever says to the mountain, 'Be cast into the sea,' and does not doubt, . . . it will come to pass. . . . Whatever you ask in prayer, believe that you will receive it, and you will." Far from being a bad moment in the otherwise compassionate ministry of Jesus, this withering of the fig tree comes to us as a word about faith, action, and prayer.

The text's denouement is presented for the first time, or better yet, hinted at. If the sermon "works" communicationally at this point, the hearers are intrigued, are provided the resource for anticipating more about the shape of the denouement, but are not yet ready to relax the tension of the conflict. The plot now moves to the "turning point."

If we are called, then, to take this fig tree story seriously, the place at which we must begin to take it seriously is precisely at the point where it rubs us the wrong way—the *injustice* of Jesus' action. It is not fair for Jesus to expect a fig tree to produce fruit out of season. *What in the name of God do you expect?*

This turns out to be precisely the question Mark wants us to ask: *What in the name of God do you expect?*

This is the turning point of the sermon plot. It comes first of all in compact, almost symbolic form—as an epiphany of sorts. In a sense, the full denouement of the sermon, the full claim of the sermon, is now present. It requires elaboration, however, before it can be integrated by the hearer.

It is the theme of the whole Gospel of Mark that
into ordinary expectations—
a new expectation was brewing.
into ordinary history—
a new and revolutionary history was bursting.
into ordinary seasons—
a new evergreen season was budding.

The very first words on Jesus' lips in Mark are: "The time is *now*, . . . the *kingdom* is at hand; repent, turn around, be revolutionized, believe in the gospel."

Mark gives us picture after picture of people whose lives had been out of season for years who, in the power of this kingdom come in Jesus, blossomed with new life and hope:

    The man in the graveyard, the village idiot—possessed by demons, crazy as hell, always had been, always would be.

What in the name of God do you expect?

    His life knitted together and made whole in Jesus. Bearing fruit out of season.

    Jairus' daughter—dead as a doornail. Hear the sounds of the wake? Weeping and wailing.

What in the name of God do you expect?

    "Little girl, I say to you, arise." And immediately, she got up and walked! Bearing fruit out of season.

    The Temple itself—so lousy with commercialism it looked like K Mart at Christmas, but the bills have to be paid, the ceremonies must be observed.

What in the name of God do you expect?

    Cleansed by the power of his word, "My house shall be a house of prayer for all the nations."

    In the power of the kingdom come in Jesus nothing which is redemptive

        just

          merciful

is *ever* out of season again!

The claim of the text is now elaborated in terms of its place in the whole Gospel of Mark.

    Weep then, not for the fig tree, but for all of us who don't know what season it is.

    Weep for the church when it expects nothing but what the world expects—a world where justice, redemption, and mercy are never in season.

    Weep for ourselves when we feel that our lives are so twisted that nothing can heal them, our enemies so hostile that we cannot love them, the poor so worthless that they are not worth our time, the world so corrupt it can never be renewed.

    Weep for ourselves when we expect only more of the same—seasons come and seasons go.

But rejoice also! Rejoice in the power of the kingdom come in Jesus! Rejoice that in the power of the kingdom come in Jesus redemption, justice, and mercy are never out of season. Rejoice in the foolishness of the gospel which calls for mountains to be cast into the sea, which invites bold prayers for righteousness, which expects fruit when the world sees only a tree out of season!

The claim of the text is moved explicitly into the contemporary situation.

Sometime ago I found myself in a conversation with a man seated next to me on an airplane, a conversation that took a rather serious turn. He told me that he and his wife were the parents of a son, now in his thirties, who was confined to a nursing-care condition for a number of years because of an injury to his brain. "We had stopped loving him," said my companion. "It's a hard thing to admit, but we had stopped loving him. It's hard to love someone who never responds. We visited him often, but our feeling for him as a son had begun to die. Until one day we happened to visit our son and discovered a visitor, a stranger, in his room. He turned out to be the pastor of a nearby church whose custom it was to visit all the patients in the nursing home. When we arrived we found him talking to our son—*as if* our son could understand. Then he read Scripture to our son—*as if* our son could hear it. Finally he had prayer with our son—*as if* our son could know that he was praying. My first impulse was to say, 'You fool, don't you know about our son?' But then it dawned on me that, of course, he *did* know. He knew all along. He cared for our son *as if* our son were whole, because he saw him through the eyes of faith, and he saw him already healed. That pastor renewed in us the capacity to love our son."

A story—a narrative picture of what the claim of the text "looks like" in one person's life—is given to make the claim concrete and to provide the hearers, through the story, with a kind of "dress rehearsal" of the claim in their own lives.

Rejoice! Rejoice that in the power of the kingdom come in Jesus even those broken in disease are never out of season in God's love.

Rejoice that in the power of the kingdom come in Jesus nothing redemptive
> just
>> or merciful is ever out of season!

The tock *of the sermon. A summary of the denouement which gives to the sermon plot the "sense of an ending."*

NOTES

1. Frank Kermode, *The Sense of an Ending: Studies in the Theory of Fiction* (London: Oxford University Press, 1967), pp. 44–45.

2. A full-length treatment of the notion of sermon "plots," from a different vantage point, can be found in Eugene Lowry, *The Homiletical Plot* (John Knox Press, 1980).

3. See Robert Scholes and Robert Kellogg, *The Nature of Narrative* (London: Oxford University Press, 1966), pp. 207ff.

4. Kermode, *The Sense of an Ending,* p. 46.

5. Leander E. Keck, *The Bible in the Pulpit: The Renewal of Biblical Preaching* (Abingdon Press, 1978), p. 113.

6. Hugh Anderson, *The Gospel of Mark,* New Century Bible (Attic Press, 1976), p. 263.

7. A. M. Hunter, *The Gospel According to Saint Mark: A Commentary* (Collier Books, 1962), p. 116.

8. Sherman E. Johnson, *A Commentary on the Gospel According to St. Mark* (London: Adam & Charles Black, 1960), p. 188.

9. Hunter, *The Gospel According to Saint Mark.*

4

Shaping Sermons by the Interplay of Text and Metaphor

Charles Rice

FORMING THE SERMON

Hans Küng has said that we get so busy dusting plastic flowers that we do not have time to cultivate roses. In preaching, this translates that we get so busy preparing sermons, we do not have time to examine them, or seek new forms for them. Yet the quest for new homiletical forms is a matter of faith—response to the gospel—and confidence in the gospel's sources, shape, sensibility, and possibilities for symbolizing itself in a way that responds to the culture and nourishes the life of the church in each age. That quest leads us to seek to design sermons which move beyond convention in order to hand over the tradition to a new generation. *What we look for in homiletics today are forms for the gospel that derive from what the gospel is, how it is communicated, and what God in Christ intends for our specific human communities.*

What criteria, then, shall we apply to sermon design? What makes a sermon recognizable and functional as a sermon? Does anything go? Are those people justified who refer to our creative efforts as "that little talk" or "your nice speech"?

Sermons *are* highly stereotyped, since the expectations surrounding the pulpit are often as unbending as Victorian table manners. There are things that simply are not done in the pulpit —that is clear—and, though it may not be so clear what they are, there are conventions which the preacher is expected to observe.

For example, it is assumed that every preacher in every sermon will do *something* with the Bible. In a church in a large southern city, a student of mine did a special project on storytelling and preaching. He found his stories everywhere and used them in various ways in the Sunday sermon. What he learned was that it didn't matter what kinds of stories he told, within certain limits of taste and propriety; the people would sit still and recognize what he was doing as preaching *if* the Bible was included in some way, shape, or form. The text might be treated quite superficially, even as a motto. That didn't matter, as long as the Bible was there.

This expectation, of course, had good historical, liturgical, and theological precedent. The earliest pictures we have of the church show the people meeting for Eucharist, reading the prophets and the memoirs of the apostles, and listening to someone expound on what was read. This image of a person opening the book and speaking is deeply ingrained in our congregations, as uninformed and unreflective as the convention may be.

It may be, too, that expectations about the style, form, and even delivery of sermons are equally strong. That is, people know what a sermon's structure is supposed to be like, the tone in which it is supposed to be spoken, the vocabulary appropriate to the pulpit, the manner and dress of someone preaching. If too many of these conventions are broken in any one sermon, communication is likely to be interrupted by the deviation itself. This does, of course, vary widely among congregations. It is likely that the structure of sermons is not something about which people are very articulate, but congregations nurtured on the three-point discourse with intermingled didactic and moralizing examples may well find departures from that pattern disconcerting.

W. D. Davies, who teaches New Testament at Duke University, once pushed his conventionalizing of preaching to the limit. Asked what he thought of the current revival of interest in preaching, Davies observed that for many persons sermons are like church bells: they are an easily recognized sound which is comforting for its familiarity and will be tolerated so long as it does not disturb early-morning sleep or some other important activity. Although Davies may be exaggerating, we certainly cannot assume —for all the links which we may forge between pulpit and the arts

—that churchgoers are as open to innovation in either sermonic form or content, as free to accept what is presented and the method of presentation, as even the same people going to the theater or the dance. Any effort to extend the number of shapes available to us for fashioning sermons has to be done in this context: most people know what a sermon is supposed to sound like, how it is to move, even how long it should be, and in what kind of voice it is best spoken.

This means, then, that *a sermon is most likely to succeed, get a hearing, if it takes its form, in whatever way or measure, from the biblical text.* The most promising direction which preaching is taking these days is our returning to the Bible unencumbered by the woodenness of earlier times, freer to bring imagination to form as well as to content. Amos Wilder led the way in the '60s, urging us to let our sermons be formed by the biblical literature itself and not to forget to bring our imaginations to the task.[1] Exegesis is a matter of *listening* to the pericope, aware of its form, refusing to speak without having deeply heard.[2] Exegesis is also a matter of *seeing,* allowing the images to live in one's own imagination. And it is a matter of *moving,* moving freely back and forth between text and context.[3] Out of listening, seeing, and moving comes the language we need.

Before making some specific proposals for forming the sermon, I will comment briefly on these three essentials of exegesis and communication.

Preaching is at least two thirds *listening:* listening to the text, to the congregation, to the surrounding culture, to oneself. The tendency is to begin talking too soon, to impose ready-to-hand ideas, "points," slogans, a sermon title, Barclay's outlines, tips from sermon aids—to lay the all too readily available language upon the text and our experience of it. We are taught, by and large, to *talk,* and the very pressure to make sermons week after week can reinforce that predisposition of academic life, to the point that *we do not do the kind of listening that enables form to spring from what is experienced.*

The first approach to sermon preparation should probably be meditation on the text, no more than an open, expectant waiting for the Bible to speak. That first movement would, I have no doubt, produce a different structure for our sermons. It is probable, too, that similar attention to the world around us would alter sermons in the same way, toward expression which springs from and stays close to experience.

As for *seeing*, literary experience is literary experience, whether one is speaking of a narrative in Acts, Isaiah's poetry, Updike's novels, or a parable. There is every chance that I will communicate to you something I have experienced *if* (1) I have in fact experienced it deeply, and (2) if in telling you about it, I stay close to the experience itself—allow myself to continue, even in the act of communication, to live in the experience. That is what happens to every good storyteller: what was experienced is experienced again, and lives in the mind's eye of the storyteller in the very act of speaking and hearing. In preaching we hope for the same thing: a literary, imaginative experience of the text which leads to the kind of expression that can close the hermeneutical circle. Our access to the text is, in the first place, by way of imagination. If we have an *experience* of the text, allow ourselves to be led deeply into its images—in our mind's eye to *see* its people, places, and things—to experience its language as a new dawning, there is every likelihood that the resulting sermon will, in form and content, rely upon and awaken imagination.

Image evokes image, story calls forth story, life speaks to life. This is the precise function of any symbol: to participate in the experience which gave it birth and to produce in the beholder/hearer a similar effect. But all of this depends upon the exegete/interpreter/preacher's capacity *to live in the symbol*, in this case in the very language and images of the text, to dwell in the house which the text provides. That capacity, an act of the imagination, is of the essence in forming sermons.

The preacher *moves* constantly back and forth between the world of the biblical story and the particular time, place, and people with whom he or she has to do, including oneself. This movement issues in the most effective sermons turning out, as Helmut Thielicke says, to be textual/thematic.[4] This ferrying between tradition and experience—ferry is a particularly good metaphor if one thinks of the ferry as constantly moving back and forth —is perhaps the most important and the most problematic aspect of the preacher's vocation.

In a team-taught course entitled "Lesson, Metaphor, and Sermon," my colleague Neill Hamilton and I have discovered that students experience real difficulty getting any kind of balance between careful exegesis of the text and equally attentive listening to the situation at hand. What has helped some students is the discipline of identifying, by both scholarly work and imagination, with, let us say, Matthew's situation. If the student is prone to be very much involved in contemporary affairs—that is, worldly— then that discipline becomes all the more important. A biblical scholar, on the other hand, would be urged to "exegete our culture." What we hope is that students will discover the mutual illumination, the interpenetration, of Matthew's real situation and ours. We have had mixed success with this, but the goal of the course—to move back and forth by both study and imagination —is of the greatest importance for the form and content of sermons. The student who does not learn how to move in both directions is very likely to produce a sermon that imposes contemporary categories and issues on the text or, conversely, a sermon that confuses exegetical information with gospel preaching. We hope that every preacher would apprehend the Bible and the world in the kind of coalescence which Frederick Buechner reveals. Waking to the morning's first rays coming in the window, he sees this as the light of creation and hears a voice saying "Let there be Buechner."[5]

If this kind of listening, seeing, and moving were achieved, then the form of sermons would, without a doubt, be closer to their actual sources in Scripture and experience. The preacher, like the artist, would be more inclined to find forms that celebrate the very thing, the living images of Bible and culture, for which there is no substitute. As Hans Küng has said:

A story cannot be replaced by abstract ideas, neither can narrating be replaced by proclaiming and appealing, images replaced by con-

cepts, the experience of being stirred, replaced by intellectual ap-
prehension.[6]

Increasingly preachers are having success with one sermon form
that is rooted in this kind of listening, seeing, and moving—the
extended metaphor. The sermon relies upon a story or an extended narrative to carry the meaning, as Jesus did in his parables.
Is there any better way to say what the story of the prodigal says?[7]

The extended metaphor or story form presupposes the ade-
quacy, indeed, the indispensability, of narrative or image to carry
meaning which has been determined to be organic to the life of
a particular Christian community. Sermons of this kind remind one
—despite the fact that they are usually longer—of the Anglican or
Roman homily, which is often a brief exegetical comment on one
of the lessons followed by a single disciplined metaphor. Various
forms enable this use of a single metaphor as the vehicle of biblical
preaching.[8]

It is possible simply to read the Scripture and then let the metaphor stand on its own beside the text. A model for this would be
Robert Raines's two books, *Soundings* and *Creative Brooding,* in
which he places alongside each other passages from the Bible and
images and narratives from literature and the media. Metaphor
interprets metaphor without explanation. Two sermons come to
mind which do this:

> Eduard Riegert preached a sermon on the parable of the great
> banquet, from which the preoccupied guests excused themselves.
> Riegert's sermon is no more than a story of Herman's coming home
> in the late afternoon, worrying over the messy house and the un-
> resolved problems of an irritating day at the office, only to discover
> too late that he has forgotten to go to his little girl's birthday party
> that very evening. Riegert lets the story stand beside Luke's account
> of the spurned supper with only a single concluding sentence to
> clinch the connection.[9]
>
> Similarly, Dana Horrell, a student of mine, preached a sermon on
> the parable of the laborers in the vineyard by reading the story and
> then telling about being first bumped by TWA, then given a first-

class seat alongside a passenger who turned out to be none too happy with the impecunious student's pleasure in wide seats, good food, and free wine. In this sermon the student included just enough phrases from Matthew's account to make the connection between the previously read parable and the extended metaphor.

In both cases, Riegert's and Horrell's metaphors proved adequate to carry the meaning that the exegete had found in the parable. The careful exegetical work that lay behind each sermon was no doubt a large part of the metaphor's linking with the text's meaning.

It is also possible to enable interplay between lesson and metaphor, and we have had various proposals for doing so. Fred Craddock's inductive method sets up a conversation between text and experience, beginning with the latter. Robert Raines preaches, as he says, "from the inside out." A typical sermon of his begins with a personal experience—in more cases than not it is precisely that, personal—and moves toward the Bible. (He is quite frank in saying that sometimes he *raids* the Bible!) Then he concludes by returning to the questions or issues or problems or things to be celebrated which surfaced in the opening experience. Metaphor and lesson merge into each other and issue in theological reflection and practical application. It is not unusual for Edmund Steimle to preach in a similar way: the politico-personal world alerts him and his hearers to a need or an opportunity which moves toward the Bible and opens toward theological expansion on the text in context. (Steimle would in every case have come to the text by way of the lectionary.) And of course Frederick Buechner's sermons are models of the interweaving of biblical language with literary and personal images. Among these preachers it is not unusual for a primary metaphor to be reinforced by a secondary image, just as in exegesis Scripture interprets Scripture. But all these preachers avoid the clutter of the merely anecdotal sermon. In all three cases it would often be possible to reduce the sermon to one lesson and one metaphor. (I suspect that the pragmatic need to fill the time available—time vacated by the neglected Eucharist?—extends many sermons beyond their optimal limits.)

In no case would the sermons of these preachers be possible apart from their biblical content.

The preaching of the black church almost invariably derives its primary metaphor from the Bible itself. I recall preaching for a black congregation at the dedication of their new building in one of the suburbs of Newark, New Jersey. I had gone there with a rather long text from II Corinthians 4–5, and an image from the movie *Question 7,* intending to elaborate the movie's picture of an East German preacher, drenched by rain pouring through the leaky roof, reading the text at hand. But when I read verse 7 of chapter 4, "For we have this treasure in earthen vessels," the congregation let me know immediately that that was the image for the day and metaphor enough. The people connected those words immediately with their new building and their experience as God's people in that place. The biblical image itself took over, as it were, the imagination of both the congregation and the preacher, within the first few minutes of give-and-take.

What would it take, by way of teaching and preaching the Bible, for the Bible's own images, its distinctive language, to function as altogether competent metaphor? That Sunday morning there was no doubt at all about the depth of meaning carried by the simple image of a clay pot; translating from "earthen vessels" to modern terms would not have heightened the meaning at all. Whatever it takes, we can only hope that the Bible will be recovered as itself metaphor, a book of imagination whose narratives and poetic language could be experienced with all the power and feeling that came flooding out in that black church.

Whatever shape the sermon takes, people who preach are moving toward consensus that *Scripture and metaphor are essentials of the sermon for our time,* whether the metaphor comes from Scripture or from outside the Bible. The shape of the sermon will vary with the lesson and the commanding metaphor, and necessarily so, since what is required is that the particular language, the concrete images, be heard and seen. The preacher's task, then, is presentation: to present the Babe lying in the manger, the Savior of the world—or, to use Wallace Stevens' image, to set before us the very object that transforms and redeems:

I placed a jar in Tennessee,
And round it was, upon a hill.
It made the slovenly wilderness
Surround that hill.

The wilderness rose up to it,
And sprawled around, no longer wild.
The jar was round upon the ground
And tall and of a port in air.

It took dominion everywhere.
The jar was gray and bare.
It did not give of bird or bush,
Like nothing else in Tennessee.[10]

Setting before us the specific images, the transforming language, is the challenge for every preacher who seeks sermon shapes appropriate to the gospel. As a teacher of mine said, if you are going to talk about a bear, it is of the greatest importance to *bring in the bear!*

The Text / MATTHEW 6:19–34
EXEGETICAL OBSERVATIONS

The sermon that follows, from the Sermon on the Mount, presents a special challenge. The passage is familiar, didactic, and—at first glance—without blatant reference to or clear dependence upon the kerygma. There is no narrative line to follow and no discernible story. A pericope of this genre is very likely to lead the preacher into contentious moralizing at worst, and at best into giving polite advice. How can exegesis and a clear intention to rely on metaphor, both within and outside the text, lead the preacher in shaping the sermon?

Matthew's situation is pertinent to ours as we meet the text. He addresses a community estranged from the religious and consequently from the economic and social establishment. Following the anathema pronounced at Jamnia, they would have ex-

perienced increasing social alienation and perhaps even economic hardship. Being made, as it were, second-class Jews, they
might well be tempted—as is many an immigrant, displaced, eth-
nic minority—to compensate by getting money and its attendant
status, at very least to try to secure themselves against an increasingly hostile world.

At the same time that Matthew's church feels its distance from
Judaism, it is defining itself as the new and true Israel. The Sermon
on the Mount, the new Torah, describes the characteristics of this
holy people. There are echoes in chapter 6 of the Beatitudes with
which the sermon begins. Here is still another picture of what it
looks like to live in the world in the consciousness of God which
motivated Jesus and which continues among his people. We have
here a profile of a disciple. As Norman Perrin has said, Matt.
6:19–34 shows us various images of the truly righteous person,
just as 7:1–12 announces various maxims illustrating the new
righteousness.[11] The proverbial sayings of 6:25–34, Rudolf Bultmann thinks, lay ready to hand for Jesus and/or Matthew to enrich
and expand them by way of sketching the disciple's profile.[12]
Bultmann remains open on the question as to whether or not these
are dominical sayings. But he thinks there can be no question that
some of this proverbial material represents popular piety, whatever use Jesus or Matthew may have made of it. Bultmann notes
that there is "no eschatological frame" for what is asked of the
disciple. Bultmann does not deny, however, that there is a tacit
presupposition of the gospel in Matthew's presentation. "Righteousness," as used in 3:15, implies the salvific event that enables
the disciple to live in single-minded blessedness.

Eduard Schweizer juxtaposes 6:19–34 with 6:1–18, where the
contrast is between the rewards which God gives and those which
man affords.[13] Sole and total devotion to God is its own reward,
and the danger in wealth does not lie in any notion that wealth
is evil in itself—the Jews had no prejudice there—but that devotion to wealth would rob one of that which was its own reward,
a single-minded devotion to God. This is the one reward that
nothing could eat away: the word could refer to the effect of

moth, rust, or worms. The call is to have one God: the metaphor of the two masters makes this clear. And this is the God who made body and life in the first place and is now revealed as the one who graciously and faithfully sustains the life of his children. This teaching, says Schweizer, presupposes the grace and mercy revealed in Jesus. The life to which Jesus calls his disciples is based on who he perceives God to be and his awareness of God's coming kingdom. It is here as with the story of the Prodigal, of which John Crossan says: "The parable is not effect but *cause* of Jesus' life and action."[14] If viewed in that way, then this *is* a Gospel pericope: we are called to trust the faithful and gracious God and to live joyfully in that trustworthy presence. This is not so much a call away from money and possessions as such, from mammon (from the Aramaic word meaning "wealth," "property") as a positive *call to remember who God is as he has been revealed in Jesus, and to live accordingly.*

The final futility, says J. C. Fenton, would be to worry about tomorrow! Anxious care could not add one yard—the metaphor is distance traveled—to our span of life.[15] The future is God's and God's alone. So we are called, by metaphor piled on metaphor, to live today much as the birds ("of the air," unclean crows?) which get fed and the lilies—grasslike narcissus they were, whose flowers scarcely exceeded one day—which are clothed more regally than even a king. The clear call of this passage, then, for our community as for Matthew's, is to live today in trusting joy, free of undue worry, available to the coming kingdom.

Sermon / ORDINARY PEOPLE

What ordinary people need, of course, is God.

The meaning that the preacher sees in the metaphor, and the theme that ties lesson to metaphor, is stated in the first sentence, but without explanation except in the presentation that follows. The question has to be faced in each sermon, to what degree and in what form the meaning will be communicated. Is the metaphor competent, apart from any specific thematic statement, to carry the meaning?

An early scene in the movie version of *Ordinary People* (Judith Guest's story of Calvin, Beth, and Conrad) takes us into the Jarretts' kitchen. Father is at the table with the paper, mother is serving breakfast, and sleepy son is down the stairs with his books. It is a sunny day and there is French toast. "Your favorite," she says. "I'm not hungry," says the boy.

Characterization begins.

Down the garbage disposal the toast, off to his law office the outwardly calm father, to the tennis court mother, and to school the teenage boy with no appetite. Do these people need God?

The theme is repeated.

About all these people do need is God!

Transitional sentence. I hope that the hearers will identify with what follows, at least not be alienated or propelled into moralistic judgments about rich and poor.

They live in a nice house, very nice, with a circular drive, off a wooded street in a suburb of Chicago. There is no want of taste or money, and by the standards of most people they live well. Yet, the white facade of their house is also a mask.

The plot begins to emerge piece by piece, as in the movie and the novel.

Connie, as they call the boy, whose brother, Buck, drowned in a boating accident two years ago, has spent time in a mental hospital after a suicide attempt so serious that the tiles of his mother's bathroom were drenched with his blood and had to be regrouted. He still has nightmares and can't eat very much. His father is cheerful and tries to keep things steady, and his mother keeps Buck's room the way it was, filled with swimming trophies and pictures of a bright blond young man. Beth goes shopping frequently and likes to travel.

The restraint intends to heighten this detail.

It would, in fact, be a mistake, in getting to know the Jarretts, to focus on their house, clothes, and accumulated travels. If, in fact, we found ourselves at one of the cocktail parties or weekend dinner parties where much of the talk is tennis and the stock market (Beth and Calvin go to these, though they don't quite want to), we would probably find the conversation familiar: food, clothing, business, "Where are you going this summer?"

Another attempt to get the hearer inside the characters' situation, to effect identification. I state what we really should not do, and then do it, since that is, in fact, what we tend to do, and it is what happens at such parties: the real agenda is obscured.

Not that we have to go to cocktail parties and stylish suppers to get into that. Beth is embarrassed at a big party with their friends when Calvin lets slip that Connie is seeing a psychiatrist. The pain and worry behind the facade and under the well-oiled conversation is a party pooper. To all outward appearances, these people have it made, but they are in desperate need,

The theme is stated again.

in need of something they cannot get with a credit card or find, as Connie puts it, "in God-damned Spain."

This prepares for the secondary story, which follows.

A friend and I saw the film at an East Side theater shortly after it opened.

An easy shift; no need for elaborate transition. In fact, just the way a movie or a novel would move us in space and time without ado.

Sitting next to us were two young people, fashionably dressed—in fact, downright chic. They supplied a second sound track; it was like seeing two movies, one on the screen and one filtered through their eyes. As the story unfolded, showing Buck and Connie out boating when a storm capsized the sailboat and the older brother was lost—our neighbors were paying close attention to the Jarretts' style of life.

More of the plot.

Connie comes home from school to an empty house; then his mother arrives, her arms full of shopping bags.

"Boy, look at those cars, color coordinated brown and black. And all that loot!"

This should set up more identification and, at the same time, disjunction, discomfort.

In another scene, the boy asks his mother if he can help her set the table; she is a perfect housekeeper and lays the table each evening with silver and linen. She tells him to go up and clean his room.

"Look at those pants . . ."

And so it went. All the superficial stuff *was* the story for my neighbors, as if this successful lawyer and his two-years grieving wife and his sleepless lean son had it made.

At points like this I would expect some movement toward the text, at least a growing readiness to hear it again.

In fact, as Calvin puts it, they might have gone on thinking themselves that they had it made, that this house and dinner at eight and Christmas in England was enough, "if there hadn't been any mess."

This should evoke, again, attraction/discomfort.

But they need God.

Theme restated.

That is not to say that these people can't cope.

Relief. Look at the positive side.

Beth certainly can: she runs a good house. You know that when they sit down to dinner, and when you watch her roll the linen napkins in their polished silver holders and put them carefully away. To be sure, having a lawyer's income helps quite a lot in coping. Someone said that the nice thing about money is that it calms your nerves.

Relief/humor.

None of the people who heard Jesus preach, certainly none of those in the community to which Matthew addressed today's Gospel, would have thought it bad that these are people of property: to say that one cannot serve God and mammon does not mean, necessarily, that wealth is bad. Far from it.

A good point to move to exegesis, and the effort here, as in the lines above, is to disarm the resistance to the usual diatribe against money and possessions.

The danger in money does not lie in any notion that wealth is evil in itself—the Jews had no prejudice there—but that devotion to wealth, undue dependence upon it, would rob us of that which is its own reward, a single-minded devotion to God:
"Let your eye be single . . ."
"A servant cannot serve two masters . . ."

Here the heart of the exegesis comes through, and the theme is sounded again, this time in close connection with the text. The language of the text is woven in.

Money can, in fact, help Beth to cope, at least to escape; it can probably calm our nerves, or at least distract us. But the call of the gospel is to have one God, and this is the God who made our body, who gave us our life in the first place, and is revealed as the one who graciously heals and sustains the children.

The integrating theme is stated again and deepened by specific theological statements.

"Therefore, do not be anxious about tomorrow . . ."
The Jarretts are not so worried about the future as fixated on the

past, as inseparable as anxiety for the future and unresolved guilt and grief from the past may be.

Their problem is described in close connection with the text. And more of the story emerges.

Connie is haunted by the thought that he might have done more, could have saved his brother. Beth—we see flashbacks of her frolicking with Buck with an abandon she does not show her husband—has pinned too many hopes on the strong, drowned boy. And Calvin, rock-like, tries to hold it all together by a determined optimism. It doesn't work. In their well-heeled, well-ordered lives, everything is in place except the past, everything under control except their grieving, anxious hearts, and consequently they are, to put it mildly, anxious about tomorrow and unable to live out even a sunny morning in a beautiful house with flowers and French toast on the table.

Returns to the opening scene.

That is because—is it not?—the fullness of every day is ours only if our eye is single, if we serve one master, the gracious God known to and in Jesus, who resolves our conflicted past, takes upon himself our guilt and grief—and gives us the future. "Not a sparrow falls on the ground without your father," is more than a statement of confidence in provision of food and clothing.

The theme is restated. Scripture interprets Scripture.

It is the confession of a gracious love that is there with us, past, present, and future, even in our mess; and so gives us today to be as fully ours, as filled with joy and beauty, as the lifting currents to a bird, the unfolding flowers of the quickly come, quickly gone narcissus.

The text's metaphors are presented, to be healing, peace-giving.

The call is to that giving up, that giving over, that single-minded opening toward the gracious God which you can see in the flower with its face turned to the sun (the very flower which tomorrow, dried and brown, may be kindling), and in the bird ("birds of the air" may well refer to the unclean crows—Jesus was no romantic about nature) which even while looking for food appears to take to the air without care.

The theme is restated by the metaphors of the text.

John Denver sings of "sweet, sweet surrender," living without care like a fish in the water, a bird in the air.

An aside, brief enough not to distract. A mere parenthesis.

It is a call to live in God, in the kingdom of God's peace and joy; and in doing that, to let everything else come in its turn and find its proper place. This is just where Matthew distinguished between those who live in Jesus Christ and the "Gentiles":

> "Do not be anxious, saying, 'What shall we eat?' or 'What shall we drink?' or 'What shall we wear?' For the Gentiles seek all these things; and your heavenly Father knows you need them all. But seek first his kingdom and his righteousness, and all these things shall be yours as well."

Would the young couple sitting next to the preacher at the movie come to mind?

The story of Beth, Connie, and Calvin is trying to tell my chic young seatmates, and you and me too, that living in God's love is life, and nothing else is.

The theme stated again, in its completed form.

But who can accept this? Who does not want to bar the door to past and future, to secure himself and surround herself, to ward off and make sure?

Save it from being glib. State the difficulty, even this late in the sermon.

When Connie finally gets up the courage to go to Dr. Berger's office, the psychiatrist asks why he has come.

Back to the story. Now that the problem is clear, and the theme is fixed, the story can have full play in finishing out the sermon, indeed in ministering to the people who have by now gotten in touch with their own pain, anxiety, and need for God's love.

Here is the place, as Paul Scherer would say, that we stop talking about love and peace and let it happen among us.

Sitting rigidly in the big overstuffed chair as if it were in his mother's proper house, Connie replies: "I want to be more in control." "I'll tell you straight, I'm not big on control," says Berger. In the months that follow, something happens to Conrad which sets him free and gives him back his life. One night, the night of his parents' return from a vacation to Texas, the boy goes into the den where they are sitting. He tells them he is glad they are home and bends to kiss his mother. She is rigid, can't let go, holds back, and the moment, the precious, eternal moment passes.

The story moves from the failure of Beth to receive love to the novel's picture of that happening, and of the peace which comes at the end.

By morning Beth has left the house, and the father and son are in the backyard. It is early and there is a chill in the air. They talk father to son, son to father, even of Buck.

> Beside him, Conrad says, "You know, I used to figure you for a handle on everything. You knew it all, even though you grew up alone, with nobody looking after you—"
>
> "I was looked after," he says. "Where'd you get that idea?"
>
> "Yeah, but nobody was responsible," he insists. "Nobody helped you with the decisions—I've thought a lot about that. I really admired you for it. I still do."
>
> "Well, don't admire people too much," he says, tossing the remains of his coffee into the bushes. "They disappoint you sometimes."
>
> "I'm not disappointed," Conrad says. "I love you, man."
>
> He winces, and his throat is tight, his eyes filled with sudden tears. "I love you, too."
>
> It is awkward, having all this between them; it bumps clumsily

against the sentences, pushing them out of meaning, out of order. Painful, the problem he has with these particular words; they threaten to overpower him, cut off his breathing. He hooks an arm around his son's neck and is at once caught in a fierce embrace. He smooths the dark head wedged against his shoulder, brushes the hair aside at the back of his neck to touch bare skin.

Conrad pulls away, straightening himself, arms on his knees, head down. "You think she'll be back soon?"

"I don't know," he says.

"You think she's coming back at all?"

"Yeah, of course!" Of course she is. *At all, God!* That is not a thought he needs to handle today. And he will not, that's that.

"She'd better," Conrad says. He wipes his hand swiftly over his eyes. "I'm a lousy cook."

Comic relief, just right at the end of this.

No need for any more words. The sun is warm on his back. He could fall asleep here, maybe he will, waiting for whatever comes next.[16]

The prayer for the day in the church year for which this Gospel is appointed makes the specifically Christological connection. A prayer of this kind, traditional words juxtaposed with a new sermon shape, is often just what is needed. The contrast is powerful.

"Most loving Father, whose will it is for us to give thanks for all things, to fear nothing but the loss of you, and to cast all our care on you who care for us: Preserve us from faithless fears and worldly anxieties, that no clouds of this mortal life may hide from us the light of that love which is immortal, and which you have manifested to us in your Son Jesus Christ our Lord; who lives and reigns with you, in the unity of the Holy Spirit, one God, now and for ever. Amen." (Collect for the Eighth Sunday after Epiphany)

NOTES

1. Amos Wilder, *Early Christian Rhetoric: The Language of the Gospel* (Harvard University Press, 1971).

2. See Leander E. Keck, *The Bible in the Pulpit: The Renewal of Biblical Preaching* (Abingdon Press, 1978).

3. See James A. Sanders, *God Has a Story Too* (Fortress Press, 1979).

4. Helmut Thielicke, *The Trouble with the Church* (Harper & Row, 1965), pp. 63ff.

5. Frederick Buechner, *The Alphabet of Grace* (Seabury Press, 1969), p. 21.

6. Hans Küng, *On Being a Christian* (Doubleday & Co., 1976), p. 547.

7. Sallie McFague TeSelle, *Speaking in Parables* (Fortress Press, 1975).

8. For one set of criteria by which to judge whether a sermon is biblical, see John Knox, *The Integrity of Preaching* (Abingdon Press, 1957), Ch. 1.

9. "Parabolic Sermons," *Lutheran Quarterly,* Vol. 26 (1974), pp. 24–31.

10. Wallace Stevens, "Anecdote of the Jar," *The Palm at the End of the Mind* (Vintage Books, 1972), p. 46.

11. Norman Perrin, *The New Testament: An Introduction* (Harcourt Brace Jovanovich, 1974).

12. Rudolf Bultmann, *The History of the Synoptic Tradition* (Harper & Row, 1963).

13. Eduard Schweizer, *The Good News According to Matthew* (John Knox Press, 1977).

14. John D. Crossan, *In Parables* (Harper & Row, 1973).

15. John C. Fenton, *St. Matthew* (London: Penguin Books, 1963).

16. Judith Guest, *Ordinary People* (Viking Press, 1976), pp. 258–259.

5
Shaping Sermons
by the Structure of the Text

William J. Carl III

FORMING THE SERMON

The Sermon as Order out of Chaos

Chester Pennington is right. God has a communication problem.[1] What we have discovered to no one's surprise is that we
who preach are part of that problem. The reasons for this conclusion are clear. We are encumbered by exegesis and theology, by
hermeneutics and church history. Some of us move cautiously
into preaching, doing our best to avoid psychologizing, moralizing, allegorizing, and harmonizing—as if we were tiptoeing
through some homiletical minefield. The result is a stifled
creativity, a muted gospel, and a paralysis that by comparison
makes the paralytic look like an Olympic champion.

On the other hand, others of us find the pressures of parish
life so demanding that we have long since forgotten about such
academic problems. The fact that Sundays keep coming, imagination dries up, and illustrations disappear creates an even
greater paralysis. No wonder God has a communication problem. But aside from our fear of the task, the seemingly insur-
mountable obstacles to communication from the pulpit, one of
our basic problems is our inability to structure our messages in
such a way that the gospel is proclaimed clearly and meaning-
fully.

Perhaps talk about structure at this point seems insignificant. If
we were to discuss it only in terms of pulpit and pew, it would be
inconsequential. What we are talking about is bringing order out

of chaos. We cannot escape a crucial theological point. God acts in the moment of preaching. Consider the beginning of Genesis where God brings order out of chaos. Does that majestic act extend to preaching? Yes, it does. In the creative act of preaching where new life is born, where the possibilities for new creation in Christ are unlimited, God certainly brings order out of the chaos of our poor words. Without this divine act of creativity we are only men and women uttering fine words to other men and women. That's not an argument for laziness or twentieth-century docetism. But without God's act of creation, talk about structure is just that—talk. Once we understand that this theological point undergirds our discussion, we can examine the significance of structure.

When I talk about structure, I am not referring specifically to the structuralist school represented by people such as Claude Levi-Strauss, Ferdinand de Saussure, Roland Barthes, or Roman Jakobson, who examine deep structures in language, literature, and society. I am talking about something at a simpler and much more basic level. I am talking about how structure is important to us in everyday life.

Most of us structure our lives with schedules and meeting times. When we see modern art, we may strain to give it symmetry—to make something out of it. The dissonance of a modern composer like Bartók or Khachaturian makes us yearn to resolve it. The same occurs with plays in the theater of the absurd, plays by Brecht, Beckett, Ionesco, Genet, or Pinter. The cognitive and emotive dissonance that their dramas create is unnerving for some.

What is at issue here is the almost innate human desire to order experiences—to bring order out of chaos in any production of speech, action, music, or light and color. Knowing deep down that in the final analysis we cannot bring true order out of the chaos of our own lives, a monumental jigsaw puzzle we will never work by ourselves, we seek some small signs of order—some glimmers of symmetrical beauty that we can know even if for only a fleeting moment. So we head for the museum or tune into a classical radio station or watch the symmetry of any finely played sport.

Because we desire order and structure, we supply it even if it's not there entirely. We hear a lecture or a sermon, and we unconsciously do our best to put together in our minds what the lecturer or the preacher is trying to say; or we tune out altogether. We try to bring order to sermons that otherwise might be without form, and void.

Playwrights, novelists, poets, movie directors all know the importance of structure. Mel Brooks has said that most movie directors spend three or four months on their scripts. He always spends a year. The script, he argues, is the raft on which everyone floats —actors, directors, camera crew, promoters. If the script is leaky, then everyone sinks. Without a tightly structured plot, the script is leaky. And so with the sermon.

Structural problems in preaching inhibit the communication of the gospel. Often after someone has preached, people will be heard saying, "Well, that was *interesting*"—a harsh indictment, for this phrase usually prefaces a critique. "But there was something wrong there somewhere. I can't quite put my finger on it." Often, the problem was structural.

At present there is a great upheaval in talk about structure in preaching. "Three points and a poem" is taking a beating. Rightly so, in some cases. Expository preaching in moderated form is seeing something of a revival. This must be comforting to Augustine and John Calvin. We still hear Harry Emerson Fosdick's problem-solution approach via Norman Vincent Peale and Robert Schuller. Not too many have resurrected the Puritan "plain style" sermon. Perhaps its predictability and terrifying length have given way to "creativity" and the twenty-minute sermon. Fred Craddock's inductive method has revived the use of illustrations that, brought together, allow the listener to hear the point.[2] Hints of Halford Luccock lurk here. But Craddock is more disciplined in his exegetical and theological interpretation.

There is also a movement in the direction of "story" or "narrative" preaching. This approach, given impetus by Steimle, Niedenthal, Rice,[3] and others, finds Scripture operating less in points and more in a variety of rhetorical forms—particularly narrative. Devotees find this structural alternative more attuned to the human process of perception. They maintain that we are born into a world of stories; we grow up listening to stories that shape our identity; we are more accustomed to and more interested in hearing stories than lectures with points. Charles Rice believes that the preacher *is* the storyteller. Therefore, the preacher's task is to help the congregation see its story in the light of the Gospel story.

The sermon itself, then, moves structurally like a story. It is not static. It goes somewhere. It wrestles with a passage creating tension and dialogue, allowing the congregation's thoughts and feelings to emerge in places. This approach emerges in David Buttrick's "moves,"[4] Eugene Lowry's "homiletical plot,"[5] and Clyde Fant's "thought-blocks."[6]

This approach seeks to take form criticism seriously. It asks what signals the passage can give as to how it wants to be preached. A parable, then, functions differently from a Pauline passage. A paranetic passage is different from an apocalyptic vision. Forcing each of these into the same structure, this approach argues, does not take seriously the variety of biblical expression.

All of these various "story" approaches have offered helpful alternatives to homiletical systems that have ignored the *form* of Scripture. They have helped us see the significance of progression —that a sermon, like Scripture, must move. They have helped us engage the congregation at deeper levels of experience in the text. They have helped us see that Scripture offers us a variety of approaches to structure.

Listening to Scripture and its different forms is like listening to music and learning to hear with a trained ear. It is like learning to hear the theme of a Bach fugue as it makes its way from part to part. Listening to Scripture and its different forms helps us realize that these forms "worked" at one time because they were based on structures that communicated, just as Bartók's music "worked" in his time because it was based on the Hungarian folk music of his day. Sometimes we find that what we do not under-

stand completely is much more highly structured than we origi-
nally thought. This is true of music and drama, and it is true of
Scripture.

My own approach to structure in preaching is eclectic. I try
different structures. I believe that the same form Sunday after
Sunday becomes predictable and comfortable to the hearers—
and can easily serve as a cure for congregational insomnia! There
are times when I find that a simple point system offers the clearest
and easiest way to communicate the gospel—to allow a certain
passage to speak. Other times I venture forth with a story form that
is dialogical and expository, i.e., that moves in and out of the text
using a whole pericope. In both, I am trying to listen to the
movement of the text and be sensitive to its tone.

Experience has taught me, however, that preaching Sunday
after Sunday, with other pastoral duties pressing down, limits the
amount of careful listening to texts that one can do. In addition,
I have discovered that sophisticated story systems and homiletical
plots can obstruct the communication of the gospel if not handled
in a disciplined manner. Without a clear logic and theo-logic
between various parts of the "narrative" sermon, the preacher
can appear to be meandering in a swamp. The parishioners are
mildly amused and entertained but lost. They leave the church
knowing something has happened, but they are not sure what. Or
they leave seeing before them a beautiful tapestry of words and
images but not the gospel.

Perhaps there is no panacea to the problem of homiletical
structure. Perhaps we put too much emphasis on this one facet
of preaching. Some preachers preach well no matter what the
structure. Others are poor despite all the right training in exegesis
and form. What makes the difference? One drama critic has said
that the problem with many modern plays is that they spend too
much time on the Emperor's clothes but have forgotten the Emperor.[7] That can apply to preaching as well. I make this assertion,
not as a retreat to piety, but as a statement of fact.

Perhaps we need to spend more time on sermon content and
our belief in it. Kurt Vonnegut has said that if you want to write,
then first have something to say, something worth saying, some-

thing about which you are passionate.[8] Kurt Vonnegut is right. You want to preach? Then first have something to say, something about which you are passionate. Never let your epitaph be, "That preacher had nothing to say, but said it well."

The Text / I CORINTHIANS 1:10–17
EXEGETICAL OBSERVATIONS

Paul probably wrote this letter from or near Ephesus on his third missionary journey. We get this information, and the fact that he had founded the Corinthian church on his second journey, only by reading The Acts. He immediately begins by addressing issues that concern him.

Paul is obviously exasperated with this congregation. A letter he had received from Corinth is not answered until chapters 7–16; he devotes chapters 1–6 to discussing reports of dissension which had come to him orally from a certain Chloe. The divisions within the Corinthian church are such serious matters that Paul gives them immediate attention. He pleads with the congregation to work out their dissensions, to see Christ as the source of their unity.

A tone of mild parental exhortation comes through the text. *Parakalō,* a contract verb from *parakaleō,* is a key word of paraenesis. It is also used in this manner in Rom. 12:1. *Parakalō* is translated by some as "please" (brothers). It connotes something between a simple request, "Pass the salt," and a divine command, "Thou shalt have no other gods before me." Paul is perturbed with his disputing children, but employs the term *adelphoi* as in his other letters: "I appeal to you, brothers and sisters. Get it together."

Yet his exasperation is expressed in personal, not public, terms. *Parakalō, erōtō, kalōs an poiēsais,* "I beseech, I request, please . . ." denote private address, whereas *deomai* and *axiō,* "I beg, I pray," belong to official communications such as letters to authorities. This philological point emphasizes the personal nature of Paul's plea. Hans Conzelmann notes further, "When a Hellenistic ruler uses the word, he is being distinctly polite: he refrains from 'commanding.' "[9]

The appeal may be personal; yet Paul makes it clear from the outset that he speaks not for himself but for Christ. It is not only because of his own pastoral concern or a certain pride for those communities he has started that he makes this request. He does so *dia tou onomatos tou kyriou hēmōn Iēsou Christou.* This heightens what Paul will say later about loyalty. His own love and loyalty for Christ lead him to this reprimand.

Paul wants no more *schismata* (splits, divisions). He wants unanimity. Orr and Walther suggest that *nous* (mind) for Paul "means the higher capacity of the human personality to be aware of God's law, purpose, and truth." Thus, to have *tō autō noï* (the same mind) is "to allow God's purpose to supersede petty motivations of human pride or prejudice."[10] The positive side of division is harmony. Paul wants all to speak with one voice.

The problem is not exactly doctrinal. Rather, people are playing favorites with leaders. Some go with the teachers Paul and Apollos. Others follow Cephas (Peter), the representative from the mother church in Jerusalem. Others comprise a Christ party, of all things. Perhaps these are Gnostics who feel superior to the other groups. Paul will not stand for these cliques.

His exhortation picks up momentum in v. 13. The *mē* in the alternate texts with "Is Christ divided?" *(mē memeristai ho Christos;)* and in the majority of texts with "Was Paul crucified for you . . . ?" *(mē Paulos estaurōthē hyper hymōn . . . ;)* indicates the intensity of Paul here. *Mē* used in a question in this manner assumes a *negative* response. "Is Christ divided?" No. "Was Paul crucified on your behalf . . . ?" Of course not! These are statements of fact, not hopes or speculations. Paul is not asking rhetorical questions open to reflection.

Christ *has not* been divided into separate proportions and parceled out—a little bit here, a little bit there. That is simply impossible. A Christ torn asunder would be unthinkable. Paul is calling all to a faith that admits no division. Division simply denies one's baptism in Christ. Is it coincidence that this passage occurs in the lectionary during the Week of Prayer for Christian Unity? Hardly.

How, then, shall we structure a sermon on this passage? One of the difficulties with preaching any Pauline text is that no narrative system appears to lead us into creativity. So we have to establish our own structure. The text itself offers its own possibilities.

Paul often operates with a kind of theological stream of consciousness. His letters seem to be spiritual outbursts, mind running ahead of pen. These Joycean outpourings frequently play logical tricks on his hearers, as in I Cor. 15:12–20.

But here the text is dialogical. It sounds forensic! There is debate among the groups; Paul debates with all of them. We can debate both Paul and the divisive groups and thus, within the sermon structure itself, attempt to retain the dialogical approach of the text. We do so with simple shifts of thought and not too many, lest the intensity of the conflict be lost.

In addition, this text moves. The exhortation is dynamic. The sermon structure needs to capture that movement. It can do so by beginning with the experience of conflict itself that lies behind vs. 11 and 12—the problem of playing favorites—and then move in and out of the passage to the Christological affirmation at the end.

In this way, theology also determines structure. The Christological move is implicit in vs. 13 and 17. It is a move that must be included to avoid salvation by works and, in this sermon, becomes the culmination of Paul's point. Usually, for Paul, theology precedes exhortation; and we act in response to God's grace as in Calvin's third use of the law. But here, the exhortation leads to Paul's belief that only in Christ can we live together in faith. Thus, the sermon may appear to operate structurally as a "problem-solution" sermon (i.e., problem = dissension; solution = Christ) but must attempt to go beyond that. We want to avoid simply saying, "Christ is the answer."

To find the controlling metaphor, we have to listen to the text. We are interested in more than what the words are saying. What are they *doing?* We immediately hear voices, the ethos of a dissonant community. The wrangling voices, the lack of harmony, the discordant sounds all suggest auditory and musical metaphors.

Echoes of politics resound in the problem of playing favorites. These merge in the sermon itself. Thus the sermon will not employ "light" illustrations or analogies as it would with John 8:12 or the transfiguration stories, or gardening examples as it could with I Cor. 3:6–9a or the parable of the sower. The only divergence from the voices is the image of the divided body in v. 13a.

Paul's entire message is pretty strong, but given with a pastoral understanding. That tone must be retained in the sermon itself. Rather than chiding or whining, this is a fervent appeal from one who believes that with Christ's help and in Christ the community will come together. The tone is not negative. But it communicates far more theologically than Peale's positive thinking or Schuller's possibility thinking. Paul believes in these people. More important, he believes in the power of God to unite them.

The title I have chosen points both to the resolution of the debate within the sermon itself and to the problem addressed by the text. It hints that on occasion God, like some cosmic composer, plans a certain amount of healthy dissonance. God's planned dissonance prevents stagnation and is more than merely a theological version of checks and balances. (See H. Richard Niebuhr's *Christ and Culture*.) But when dissonance is unplanned, when it happens as a result of our own self-centeredness, cacophony results and problems arise. Only in Christ does true harmony occur.

Sermon / UNPLANNED DISSONANCE

No doubt many of you have watched with great interest this year's presidential primary results. You have cheered the victory or lamented the defeat of your candidate. Since preachers should steer clear of explicit mention of politics in the pulpit, my own candidate from Tennessee shall remain nameless. It doesn't matter much anyway now since he's out of the race, as are most of the others. One thing is clear, though. Our loyalty to these candidates sometimes finds us putting them on pedestals and treating them as heroes.

This is simply a way of getting into the idea of favorites.

The same is true in the church, isn't it? We have our favorites here as well. We may scorn the idea of sainthood, but we have our heroes in the faith, just the same. There's John Calvin, or Martin Luther, or maybe a famous preacher we've heard—a George Buttrick or a Peter Marshall. For some, it's a famous evangelist or religious television personality. It may be some preacher we have known from our childhood, someone we looked up to or even possibly feared. Perhaps it was someone who held our hand when our mother or father died, or even a spouse.

Into the passage with a touch of politics.

Whatever the case, the fact is that both in politics and in the church we set up our loyalties and stick by them.

I deal with background here and two paragraphs later to help create tension.

Well, loyalties existed in the early church too. Peer in on Corinth, a little Greek town not far from Athens, once a flourishing city, now just another whistle stop on Paul's campaign trail. Yet Paul had a special fondness for the church in this town—he had helped found it. In Ephesus he hears from Chloe, possibly a wealthy woman in whose house the Corinthians used to meet; through her report comes the friction, the bickering, the house he loves divided against itself.

It is not surprising that the strains of hymns such as "The Day of Resurrection" and "Jesus Christ Is Risen Today" were still echoing throughout the church when these wrangling cries arose, almost like a chant, not too different from that Good Friday chant. Somehow, "Crucify him, crucify him!" had merged into, "Paul! Apollos! Peter! Christ!" Almost as if there had been no empty tomb, no unlikely stranger on the Emmaus road.

Here I am setting up the tension that exists in the text itself. I usually do not offer this much background, but here it seems appropriate.

Four different groups had arisen. How similar they sound to some in our own day! The Paul group stressed Christian freedom. Paul had been called and taught by God, not by any human. There was something rough and passionate about his speech, and those who followed him were the same. The Apollos group loved philosophy and eloquence, since their leader was refined, polished, a man who knew both the world and the Scripture and was an orator *par excellence.* The Peter group probably put stock in church authority and organization.

As Jewish Christians who still clung to much that was Jewish, they were no doubt slow in understanding God's love toward the Gentiles. Some say that the Christ group perceived themselves as superior to others because of their personal devotion to Christ. They may have prided themselves on their spirituality and claimed a direct communion with God. We might even call them the "Me and Jesus Group." What has happened to that idyllic picture in Acts 2 of happy disciples frolicking about, praising God, stumbling into the river to be baptized, breaking bread in gleeful agape feasts, down on their knees in prayer, full of hope for the coming kingdom? Somehow, here in Corinth the picture has been marred.

But before we make too much of the dissension, let me be so bold as to say that difference in the church can be very good. We make a lot out of our different denominations, naming all the splits and schisms with great lament.

First shift in thought. In a pastoral problem like this one, I find that a touch of humor helps release some of the tension. Bonnell provides that.

John Sutherland Bonnell once listed some of the variations in the Baptist Church in the early part of this century. Among others, there were the Northern and Southern Conventions, the American Baptist Association, the Duck River and Kindred Associations, the General Six-Principle Baptists, the Free Will Baptists, the Separate Baptists, the Regular Baptists, the Primitive Baptists, and last but not least, the Two-Seed-in-the-Spirit Predestinarian Baptists. Somehow the name "Presbyterian" pales by comparison. He also points out that in the Church of God, a branch broke off calling itself the True Church of God, and then another called the Only True Church of God.[11]

Certainly we've had splits in our church too; we know this all too well. But sometimes doctrinal differences can add richness to a church.

I present some evidence of healthy divergence of opinion.

Raymond Brown, in his Sprunt Lectures at Union Seminary in Richmond, Virginia, pointed out that doctrinal diversity in the New Testament churches was in some ways very healthy. By themselves, different churches represented in the New Testament were limited. Each was calling the other heretics. Interestingly, no group ever calls itself heretical. But each group saw part of the truth about Christ and his church. None saw the whole. What kind of Jesus do we find in the New Testament? Matthew's Jesus, who says, "Love your enemies," among other things; the Marcan Jesus, who suffers; the missionary Jesus in Luke; the Jesus who was before all and knew all in John; the High Priest Jesus in Hebrews; and the great vision in Ephesians of the church as the mystical body of Christ with Christ as the head. Each group saw part of the truth about Christ and his church. But the New Testament as a whole gives the fuller picture.

Here I dialogue with Paul. I allow the congregation's questions to emerge. Evidence of wrestling with the text creates conflict and heightens interest.

So when Paul says to the Corinthians to be of the same mind, we have to raise a question. Certainly he can't mean thinking the same thing. Sometimes being of the same mind can be limiting and very boring. Does the Lord want little automatons all thinking the same thing? How dull a church that would be. Differences can create richness. Some have argued that the problem with presbytery meetings is that they are so dull. You never get into good theological debates over things that really matter, the way presbytery meetings were supposed to be when our Scottish forefathers initiated them. Thus, the church grows staid and stagnant. As long as we meet as brothers and sisters in Christ, we have the right to disagree over things that *really matter.* Not like the church in Pennsylvania that has been split for years because years ago one group wanted to have a sauerkraut dinner for a church night supper and another group didn't, and the two groups haven't spoken to each other since. Now that might be something worth arguing over, but it is certainly not something to remain speechless about for years.

Here I am using the musical metaphor to illustrate.

When the choir sings, it often sings different parts, but the same piece, all working from different perspectives to present a richer, fuller whole. The tenor by itself, or the alto alone, would sound odd, except in a solo. In the same way, composers add dissonance to their music to create richness and texture, because they know that total consonance eventually becomes boring. As in a good marriage or a deep friendship, so also in the church, the right to disagree enriches our relationships. A real friend is a "person with whom you can disagree, knowing that mutual respect and affection are not at stake."[12] Yes, differences can be good.

Significant shift in thought occurs here.

And yet, they can also be destructive. How well we know this side of the story. In Corinth, the differences were not merely doctrinal but personal. The groups had become closed, pushing their own positions to the exclusion of others'. The right to disagree had been lost. The existence of the congregation itself was threatened. The church consisted of factions and not believers in Christ. Each group was lobbying for its own rights. Somehow that fractured picture is repeated today.

From sermon preached at Union Seminary, Good Friday, 1980. It helped make the point.

Steve A. Martin once noted that in the Presbyterian Church in the United States "every group affirms its right to the whole picture, the big picture. The quest for the common good is lost behind a rhetoric of increasing intensity. . . . There is a women's caucus, a Black caucus, the Texas Mafia, the Virginia gentility, and the

North Carolina good ole' boys. And the PCUS, that once gathered in Montreat to pray and praise and celebrate its oneness in Jesus Christ, is getting together in Myrtle Beach to set goals." What is the matter with us? Can you hear the echo of our own voices, "It's my church!" "No, it's mine!"

Paul's exasperation comes through here: "Baptism is only in one name. Don't follow me. My loyalty is to Christ."

You can almost hear Paul in the background cajoling his Corinthian congregation, "Were you baptized in the name of your factions?" "Did your factions go to Calvary for you?" When we dispute too much in the church, not speaking the truth in love, Paul's voice rings like a haunting refrain, "Is Christ divided?" Has Jesus become some giant jigsaw puzzle we'll never be able to work?

As a preacher, I take a risk with the mixed metaphor.

To change the metaphor, when dissonance is unplanned, it becomes only cacophony—as if for the last hymn each of you turned to a different number and began singing.

Final shift of thought into the Christological move.

What is at stake here, for us as for Paul, is that without Christ the church doesn't exist. The goal is to bring all together by bringing them back to Christ.

So what can we do? We can turn our ears from the voices of factions and listen for the lone Judean's voice which lifts us out of our self-centeredness into a new oneness. Beyond the cries of "Crucify him, crucify him," beyond the Good Friday silence, we hear his voice strong and clear over our shoulder on the Emmaus road, or, like Mary Magdalene, we hear him calling us by name.

Here I want to demonstrate the futility of human endeavor to achieve unity. Christ is our only hope.

And hearing his voice helps our voices come together. Somehow all our Babel voices come together in him. We certainly don't get together on our own. We should know that by now. Sooner or later, we learn a very simple fact. Not all ecclesial schizophrenia can be solved by simply listening to the other side or deciding to be good friends, like it or not; or appealing to our common humanity; or even voting for church union. In the end, all of these fall short. Only because of Christ do we get together and do what we do in this building. Think about it. In worship we pray and sing with those we would normally ignore on the street. In communion we sit at table with those we would not normally invite to our homes for dinner. Why? Because of Christ.

I continue the musical metaphor to the end.

In Chicago every year around Easter, three thousand people get together, bringing their own scores, and sing Handel's *Messiah.* People from all walks of life, some from various churches, some not, some who sing well, some only mediocre, raise their voices to the King of Kings and the Lord of Lords. Interviews with a random few were very revealing. One particular man said: "It sends chills up and down your spine to hear so many sing *The Messiah* together. There's a marvelous coming together that occurs here, as it does in no other way."

How appropriate that the Messiah should bring so many people together. Of course, he always has, hasn't he?

NOTES

1. Chester Pennington, *God Has a Communication Problem* (Hawthorn Books, 1976).

2. Fred B. Craddock, *As One Without Authority: Essays on Inductive Preaching* (Phillips University Press, 1974).

3. Edmund A. Steimle, Morris J. Niedenthal, and Charles L. Rice, *Preaching the Story* (Fortress Press, 1980).

4. David G. Buttrick, "Interpretation and Preaching," *Interpretation,* Vol. 35, No. 1 (Jan. 1981), pp. 46–58.

5. Eugene Lowry, *The Homiletical Plot* (John Knox Press, 1980).

6. Clyde E. Fant, Jr., *Preaching for Today* (Harper & Row, 1975), pp. 122–123.

7. Robert Anderson, "Thoughts on Playwrighting," in *The Writer's Handbook,* ed. A. S. Burack (The Writer, 1976), p. 482.

8. Kurt Vonnegut, *Palm Sunday* (Delacorte Press, 1981), pp. 77–78.

9. Hans Conzelmann, *A Commentary on the First Epistle to the Corinthians* (Fortress Press, 1975), p. 31.

10. William F. Orr and James A. Walther, *I Corinthians* (Doubleday & Co., 1976), p. 150.

11. John Sutherland Bonnell, *Fifth Avenue Sermons* (Harper & Brothers, 1936).

12. William Sloane Coffin, Jr., *Once to Every Man* (Atheneum Publishers, 1977), p. 132.

6
Shaping Sermons by the Shape of Text and Preacher

Gardner Taylor

FORMING THE SERMON

The initial issue for structuring sermons is the preacher's own faith about Scripture. If one sees Scripture as being word for word, accent by accent, incident by incident, genealogy by genealogy, the precise word of God, then the sermon is likely to take on a quality of *ex cathedra* pronouncement. This leaves little room for the sermon to muse upon any human traits and insertions that offer an earthy, credible point of association for the lives of those who sit in the pews. On the other hand, if the preacher believes little more about the nature and meaning of the Scriptures than that they are the most elevated human literature, then the sermon is likely to ignore the mysteries of God's self-disclosures and people's uneven responses to those disclosures which are the very kernel of biblical material. A sermon has the greatest chance of accomplishing its proper hoped-for and prayed-for purpose in human life when it arises out of the preacher's own faith that in the words of Scripture a Word arises.

It was along this line that P. T. Forsyth spoke in his 1907 Lyman Beecher Lectures at Yale. He said: "I do not believe in verbal inspiration. I am with the critics, in principle. But the true minister ought to find the words and phrases of the Bible so full of spiritual food and felicity that he has some difficulty in not believing in verbal inspiration." There is a sense in which the Bible has a life of its own which must be recognized. There is a continuing thought of the Bible, a theme which will deliver the sermon from being merely some thoughts *about* Scripture and which will make it a part of the thought of the Bible itself.

A second issue for structuring sermons concerns the person of the preacher. Some texts lend themselves more cordially to one preacher than to another. This is not to say that one must hop and skip through the Scriptures looking for sermon texts that suit the preacher's personality. But the truth is that the coloring and texturing of the sermon, no matter what the text may be, will be influenced by the personality and outlook of the preacher. Nor is this to be frowned upon, since our own personalities are the only true currency in which we may deal authentically with those who hear us.

It is a glory of preaching that one text can be given as many different nuances—all of them loyal to the Scriptures—as there are preachers dealing with them. In my years in the City of New York some of the most notable preachers of our generation have been my colleagues, and their memories are still a benediction to me. How different they were and how gloriously did those differences come out in their pulpit work! A sermon of Robert McCracken's invariably reflected the wistful, gently probing makeup of the preacher. In George Buttrick's sermon, one always detected a pursuing logic, a care about simple but eloquent diction and a brooding upon the mystery of godliness and life which were a slice of that preacher's being. Adam Clayton Powell was saucy in temperament and intensely angry about injustice; he also had a lofty concept of Scripture, inherited from his father. Bring those elements together with an almost hypnotic voice, and the resulting sermon is fiery, prophetic, and deeply stirring—particularly to those most closely associated with injustice and hopes long deferred. Paul Scherer was grand and expansive in personality, so his sermons were spacious, sweeping, almost Shakespearean in imaginativeness. The Brooklyn preacher Sandy Ray had a warm, infectious disposition and a genius for finding in Scripture fresh angles of vision often gained from shrewd observations of the human scene. No matter what text he preached, one could see these qualities in his sermon.

As preachers vary, so their sermons vary in what is highlighted and in the way the sermon gets at the minds and hearts of the hearers. The preacher needs to consider himself or herself in relation to the text, whatever it may be, in order to guard against attempting, on the one hand, what is unnatural, and on the other hand, what is merely eccentric.

A third issue for structuring sermons is the intent and type of passage chosen for the text. Almost always a sermon must move within the intent and atmosphere native to that particular passage. Doubtless there are times when legitimately the sermon may give a passage a meaning that it does not have in its original setting and purpose. For instance, Harold Cooke Phillips, the highly regarded Cleveland preacher of the 1930s and 1940s, had a memorable sermon on "The Angel in the Sun" from Rev. 19:17. The sermon made no attempt to deal with the text contextually, but he declared himself in this regard at the very outset, and it was a splendid sermon by a master craftsman. Yet even in Phillips' hands, the sermon was weakened because the central underpinnings of the text's scriptural supports seemed removed.

Far worse is a sermon in which the text is tortured out of its original meaning and in which an obviously wrong use of it is made. This reveals either dishonesty or ignorance—or both. Yet one hears sermons now and again which valorously violate the original meaning of the text, but carry great power and persuasiveness. The late Dr. Marshall Shepard of Philadelphia spoke of a certain thriving church in his city as having been "gloriously built on wrong preaching." Someone has reported having heard a sermon of inquiry into problems of the resurrection posited upon a completely wrong treatment of I Cor. 15:13: the trumpet blast was changed into a query, and the sermon sallied forth with the question, "Now is Christ risen from the dead?"!

One pondering a sermon ought to look at the text in its setting and surroundings. A wise preacher of another generation suggested that one ought to "walk up and down the street on which a text lives." The surrounding terrain ought to be taken into account. What is the block like on which the text is located? Is it a run-down section, or does it sparkle with a neat tidiness? Is the sky overhead leaden or gray, or is it bright and sunlit? Does one hear light and merry music in the neighborhood of the text, or are there solemn cadences of some sad and mournful time? One need not get lost in atmosphere, but a sense of climate will greatly aid the sermon in breathing with life and having, therefore, an interest for living people.

As an example of that kind of preaching nobody in our time surpasses the engaging Riverside Church preacher, William Sloane Coffin. Nobody can argue about Dr. Coffin's interest in the largest and most disputed issues of our time as they relate to the will of God. At the same time, his touch for detail is superb. No one who heard his sermon at the Fosdick Convocation on Preaching can forget his trenchant and prophetic condemnation of militarism. The force of that sermon was greatly secured by Dr. Coffin's imagining of Goliath haughtily looking for the first time on young David and dismissing him with the sniffing question, "And who is this lad with those stones?" Again, at Emory University, Coffin dealt with the paralytic man who was let down through the roof of a house so that Jesus might heal him. Dr. Coffin commented that a fitting first command to the healed man might have been, "Now repair this roof!" How arresting!

More often than not, the structure of a sermon can be determined by the movement of the text itself. Some of us like to look upon the sermon as a journey. We start with some sense of goal: To what part of the life in Christ is it that we want to point and lead the worshipers? We then seek a point of origin and a path, a roadway, by which we hope to arrive at the city that is the destination of that sermon's pilgrimage. Incidentally, this concept can greatly assist those who would like to develop some skill in preaching without manuscript. Some texts especially lend themselves to such a method, even seem to mandate such a procedure. Job 19:25–26 is one such passage in its sense of direction and movement. There is affirmation that "my Redeemer liveth." This is not static truth, it moves on to his appearance, "and he shall stand . . . upon the earth." And so there is "one far-off divine event, to which the whole creation moves," no matter what forces of history or history's people may stand against it. The soul, stripped and straining to catch sight of that fulfillment, cries out in stubborn faith, "Yet in my flesh shall I see God." In such preaching the text is the sermon contracted and the sermon is the text expanded.

There are other texts that suggest a structure of antithesis, a quality often seen in the incandescent pulpit work of Frederick W. Robertson. The Old Testament scholar-preacher James A. Sanders made powerful use of this bipolar way of preaching in a sermon delivered at Union Theological Seminary. Intriguingly titled "In the Same Night . . . ," the sermon is contained in the text: "It was on the night in which we betrayed him that he broke bread and gave it to us," said the preacher. "Betrayed," "broke bread . . . and said, Take, eat."

A sermon's structure or design may be by way of negatives, a kind of sermonic counterpart of the "via negative" method that Eastern Orthodox theologians use in reflecting on the attributes of God. One example of such a text is a portion of the fifteenth chapter of I Corinthians. Paul approaches the trumpet blast "Now is Christ risen from the dead" by way of some solemn and terrifying negative suppositions. I have called them Paul's "domino theory" of consequence in the event that the resurrection is lost to Christian faith. "If Christ be not risen, then is our preaching vain, and your faith is also vain . . . and we are found false witnesses . . . ye are yet in your sins . . . they also which are fallen asleep in Christ are perished . . . we are of all men most miserable." Each possibility sounds a new dirge of despair before the shout of victory "Now is Christ risen from the dead, and become the firstfruits of them that slept." One sees strong traces of this method of preaching in the sermons of Frederick W. Robertson and James Stewart. Stewart used the very passage above in a deeply moving sermon on the resurrection.

Whatever the structure, a sermon must deal with two things: the "revelant" (to use Kyle Haselden's fine term) and the "relevant." The Bible speaks of a beginning, a quest, a choosing, an emancipation, a journey, a nation, an exile, a restoration, and the appearance of One who incarnates all of that and all that God intends. This is the "revelant," and this record—punctuated by the pronouncements of the prophets—is more than a book of texts. It is the preacher's textbook. Life offers to preacher and hearers the individual concerns all people have and the agelong attempts they have made to establish some form of community. Attempts to contract community repeatedly produce tensions of class, section, race, creed, the threat of war, and, now, of annihilation. This is the "relevant." The sermon's task is to swing the light of proclamation, not mechanically, from what is "revelant" to what is "relevant," to show how one touches the other and the demands made in the name of the Sovereign Lord of them both.

In structure, design, and delivery the sermon ought to breathe with the awareness that it is doing business in the supreme matters of human life. It ought not to be trivial nor fancy nor syrupy nor mean nor truckling to any human pride or pretense. It ought to be a word "as from a dying person to dying people," to paraphrase Richard Baxter of Kidderminster. Every sermon, as B. L. Manning put it, ought to be "a manifestation of the Incarnate Word from the Written Word by the spoken word."

It would perhaps not be improper in conclusion to set down some indicatives which I have gleaned over the years from the strange art of preaching. A sermon usually has a better chance in our biblically illiterate time if it begins with a "cool introduction" in which the secret, or purpose, of the sermon is suggested but not exposed. Such an introduction ought to touch the hearers at a point of concern or interest in their lives. The sermon must then get down to the hard business of making intelligible its purpose, all the while making honest allowance for the doubts and exceptions that may be occurring in the minds of the hearers because they have already occurred in the mind of the preacher. Then having earnestly, honorably, and candidly advanced the purpose for which that sermon has been called into life, the preacher ought to try to bring the people before the presence of God and within sight of the heart of Christ. No sermon can do more. None should want to do less.

The Text / I CHRONICLES 10:13–14
EXEGETICAL OBSERVATIONS

The problem for Chronicles and, of course, for I Chron. 10: 13–14, is that of looking back on an event with the inescapable bias of the viewer. Brevard Childs says that one of the "most difficult theological problems of the canonical approach to the Old Testament involves understanding the relationship between the divine initiative in creating Israel's scripture and the human response in receiving and transmitting its authoritative Word. Christian theology has, by and large, continued to describe the Bible in traditional terminology as the 'Word of God' which implies divine authorship in some sense. Nevertheless, few theologians in this post-critical era would wish to deny that the active human participation in the hearing, writing, and transmission of the Bible is an absolutely necessary feature for correctly understanding the text."[1]

The writer of Chronicles has been charged with being lopsided in his presentation of the history of the Israelite people. Quite obviously the writer has used Samuel and Kings as a source; some scholars are of the opinion that there was another source which we do not have. The author does have an ulterior purpose, since there is no such thing as pure history or pure anything else. The more pertinent questions are whether the author's ulterior purpose is worthy, and whether he seeks to reach that purpose by honorable means.

The writer of Chronicles is setting down history with an upward look. He looks back from the fourth century B.C. at the events of the nation and sees in them the purposes of God being fulfilled. Werner Lemke says that the principal question here is "not between original event and Biblical record but between the earlier tradition in the text of Samuel–Kings and the Chronicler's reshaped composition. The writer raises the question of how Israel's sacred historical tradition functioned authoritatively for the continuing life of the people of God."[2] So, the writer aims to show continuity of the eternal covenant running through David to the days of the restored Temple in Jerusalem.

One also finds an ethical emphasis in Chronicles which asserts that the eternal covenant demands of God's people an obedient response and recognition of the legitimacy of the postexilic priesthood and the Jerusalem Temple. "Very telling in this regard is the image of David contrasted with David in Samuel; the man of war, astute politician, loving father and wise judge of the earlier work is lost behind a portrait of David as head of the church and surety for messianic hopes. The Chronicler viewed Judaism as a community of living belief, not as a national cult. The Chronicler reviewed history and found it to lead with divine purpose to the moment and place where he himself stood within the Temple precincts, all indications to the contrary notwithstanding."[3]

Saul then is cast by the Chronicler as a villain, since his reign is a prelude—and a grim one, too—to the golden era of David. The Chronicler faces the problem of how to account for the nation's times of disaster and humiliation; therefore he emphasizes how, through Saul, the kingdom turned in the wrong direction—all the more saddening because Saul showed such brilliant promise in the beginning days of his rule. It has been said of Isaiah Berlin, the novelist, that he has the gift to clothe ideas with personality. In the Chronicler's depiction of Saul, the nation is personified. Saul goes down and the nation goes down, notwithstanding the fact that each exists by the express will of God.

The difference between the perspective of the writers of Samuel and Chronicles is highly evident in the difference between their accounts of the death of Saul. In I Samuel 31, Saul's death is told as part of the story of a vast military defeat. In I Chronicles 10 the writer feels a need to give theological reasons (with political overtones) for the king's death. In the sight of the Chronicler, Saul died for one reason: his unfaithfulness to God. And to make certain that the reader understands the depth of that unfaithfulness, the writer gives specifics: "He did not keep the command of the LORD, and also consulted a medium, seeking guidance." Because the Chronicler begins his narrative text with Saul's final battle, none of the illustrative stories referred to here are actually contained in I Chronicles itself. But three incidents described in I Samuel contained what the writer considered the seed and root of Saul's end, elements that would have been extremely important for this post-exilic writer. The record of Saul usurping the priestly function (I Samuel 13) underscores the importance of the priesthood. The record of his failure to obey God's explicit command in the matter of the Amalekites—a failure that led Samuel himself to declare "to obey is better than sacrifice, and to hearken than the fat of rams" (I Sam. 15:22)—fits the Chronicler's insistence that the covenant demands strict obedience by God's people. And the story of Saul's attempting to invoke the presence of Samuel's ghost at the cave of the witch of Endor suggests several things that would be greatly important in postexilic times.

And so, for the Chronicler, Saul appropriately comes to an ignominious end. His reign serves as a dark and solemn backdrop for the Chronicler's presentation of the bright, brilliant era of David, with his responsibility for the emphasis on the Temple and all that that represents.

Sermon / A SAD MEMORIAL

Words spoken by my college president, Dr. John Alvin Bacoats, ring increasingly in my ears across the years. Over the wide gulf of time that separates then from now, that good man's words shine forth in my memory. One of the things he often said to us was, "What you are today will largely determine what you will be tomorrow."

A familiar, a tender, or an instructive recollection steadies the preacher in those uncertain first minutes of preacher-congregation engagement.

Now, this is not to say that tomorrow cannot be different from today. He said, rather, that tomorrow is largely, not solely, shaped by today. To be sure, tomorrow can be different. We can change. Old habits can be beaten and banished from us. The grip of a bad disposition can be broken, and ugly ways can be transformed. It is not altogether true that you cannot teach old dogs new tricks. Old dogs are learning new tricks every day—how to walk slower, bark lower, and scratch harder. We have got to stop letting ourselves off with our bad manners and impolite attitudes by saying: "I have been like this for thirty or forty years. It is just my way." Well, it is the wrong way and you and I ought to be ashamed of being nasty, brutish, unfeeling, and savage in the way we talk to each other. We can do better.

Still, there is a gathering power that belongs to habit. Things repeated tend to become fixed. The child repeats a piece of poetry until it is fixed in the memory. An athlete repeats a motion until it enters what they call "muscle memory."

I try to have people know that the sermon has to do with their day-to-day development into whatever it is they are at last to be, irrevocably.

In this sense my old college president spoke a profound truth. Tomorrow is not the slave of today, but heaven knows it is the servant; it is not the brother or sister, but nothing farther out than first cousin. You young people who hear me today ought to take to mind the lesson that you are laying now the beams and substructure, the foundations and underpinning of character which will affect all the rest of your lives. Some of us have learned to our regret, and sometimes to our doom, that poor habits of study, of concentration, of attention, of self-discipline become giants and we in their presence, like the spies sent forth to survey Canaan, are "in our own sight as grasshoppers." Having allowed this habit, that slovenness to get a foothold in our lives and a stranglehold around our willpower, we are slaves who were meant to be masters. Remember! What you are today will largely determine what you will be tomorrow.

It is with this in mind that I would repeat "the sad memorial" which the writer of I Chronicles lifted up over the memory of Israel's first king, Saul.

I am unfailingly touched by the direct, unerring way in which the Bible cuts to the heart of things. It is not

Here there is attempt to make certain that the Bible sets forth the sermon's idea and intention.

a book of unnecessary detours, loose language, cloudy meanings. This brave old book calls things by their true title. The Bible tells it like it is. In this book night is night and day is day, sin is sin, hell is hell, and God is God. It does not attempt to prove things to be true, it proclaims things that *are* true. Characteristically, then, the Bible rears this monument over King Saul: "So Saul died for his transgression which he committed against the LORD, even against the word of the LORD, which he kept not, and also for asking counsel of one that had a familiar spirit, to inquire of it; and inquired not of the LORD: therefore he slew him, and turned the kingdom unto David the son of Jesse."

What a horrible epitaph! We would not put that on the tombstone of our worst enemy. But the Bible states it baldly, boldly, clearly, starkly—shall I say brutally? "Saul died for his transgression which he committed against the LORD."

It did not have to be that way. Looking back from this last awful word to Saul's early bright promise, we see how sad and progressive was the fall of this man who was king.

The sermon goes back from the text where Saul ends to the bright promise of his beginning and tries to find the path that brought him to ruin.

What solemn lessons the word of God gives us as we look at Saul's start and Saul's finish. The tragedy, the sorrow of it all, becomes deeper and darker as we see the path that brought this king down and left his name at last shrouded in disgrace and stained with shame.

Saul had marvelous natural gifts. He looked the part of a king. He was tall in stature, noble in bearing, and regal in manner. Saul came to his throne at an opportune and promising time politically. The people were hungry for a king, and Samuel, who had been judge in Israel, was old and weak, his own sons godless and grasping. Saul came to his throne with the blessing of Samuel the Judge and apparently with some of Samuel's affection.

Perhaps Samuel saw in Saul the appearance of what he wished for in a son. Saul was brave in battle and admired by those around him. He was blessed with children, and one of them—Jonathan —was a lad of rare and noble quality. Add up these things and the tragedy of the epitaph, the sadness of the memorial which The First Book of the Chronicles raises over Saul becomes all the more terrible and sad.

I attempt to establish a contrast between what promise Saul had at the outset and how the Chronicler describes his finish. This is by way of opening interest as to how this happened.

How and why did this man who was so endowed, so equipped, come to such an end?

Saul failed to heed sound and godly advice. Samuel favored him, and again and again told Saul what God wanted him to do. There were two incidents that illustrate Saul's turning from the will of God as it came to the king through Samuel, the aged and honored judge in Israel. In the first instance, Samuel told Saul not to move against an enemy for seven days, until Samuel could come to offer sacrifice. For whatever reason (for the mind of God is so far above ours that it sometimes seems ridiculous—that being "the foolishness of God" of which Paul speaks in I Corinthians), Samuel told Saul that God's will was that Saul should wait seven days before entering the battle, until Samuel came to Gilgal and made a sacrifice before God for the people. But Saul grew impatient when Samuel did not appear at the precise moment agreed to, and so Saul offered the burnt offering himself.

Was this the first case of a political person appropriating the acts of religion in service of the state—the beginning of civil religion?

Here the attempt is made to expose the relevance, the contemporaneity, of what Saul did about making religion a tool of statecraft.

The altar of religion and the rostrum of state ought never be so close that the sounds coming from one are indistinguishable from the sounds coming from the other. At any rate, when Samuel appeared, apparently having walked the fifteen miles from his home in Ramah to the battle site at Gilgal—Gilgal, the same city beneath which Saul had once knelt to receive the anointing as king of Israel —when Samuel arrived and learned that Saul had already offered the sacrifice, Samuel did not commend Saul, but said rather: "Thou hast done foolishly: thou hast not kept the commandment of the LORD thy God. . . . Thy kingdom shall not continue."

There was another incident where Saul discounted and disobeyed the warning of God as it came through the lips of Samuel. The Amalekites who fought against Israel were all to be wiped out, including their cattle and other holdings. We raise our eyebrows at what seems to us an awful and savage command. We shudder at the order to wipe out and to destroy. Yet thus it stands. We can but read this barbarous injunction in terms of the times in which it was uttered. And when the battle was over, Saul failed to obey what God through Samuel commanded him to do. Not for humanitarian reasons did Saul spare the livestock of the Amalekites, but for greed and gain. Oh, Saul claimed to Samuel that he spared the sheep and oxen in order to make sacrifice to God. But Samuel replied with a word that still stands as a high-water mark of ethical religion: "Behold, to obey is better than sacrifice, and to hearken than the fat of rams. . . . Because thou hast rejected the word of the LORD, he hath also rejected thee from being king."

I shift here to application.

Here is a solemn lesson. All of us have received at some place or another a clear word as to what God would have us to do. All of us have the influences of God playing upon our lives. All of us have heard the call, "Repent, believe, and be baptized."

God's word comes to us in so many forms. The Scriptures speak to us of God's dealing with his people through countless generations and innumerable centuries which are now gone but whose lessons are still stark and clear; we ought to hear God's word through Scripture. Our consciences are the sentinels of our souls, and they cry out to us in hours of testing and temptation; we ought to hear God through our conscience. Our parents and elders have gained wisdom by virtue of their years and experience; we hear God through their admonitions. In our nation, we hear God as we look back upon and take lessons from what is noblest in our national heritage in terms of our great political concepts of freedom, opportunity, and human worth. God speaks in many ways. But Saul failed to hear God's word.

Saul failed at another point, too. Here was a man in whom there was so much good and so much bad, so much strength and so much weakness, so much kindliness and so much cruelty that we feel great sympathy for him. Though he was rebellious and disobedient, Samuel, the old judge, mourned for him so deeply that God had to remind Samuel to sorrow no more for Saul.

Saul's quirks of personality offer opportunity to delve into what is interior about the king and to show how similar we all are.

We, too, are drawn to him, maybe because the mixtures in him make him so human. He spared his worst enemy, Agag, and was ready to kill his best friend, David. He was kind and yet cruel. He was rash in danger and cautious in safety. Music could move him to tears and a religious ecstasy that left him limp on the ground, yet the storm could grow so violent in his soul that he was like a madman.

As in all of us, an angel and a devil wrestled in Saul's soul. But Saul allowed what was lowest in him to get the upper hand. Jealousy, envy, and pride drove him to seek David's life. Fear and ambition swept him along on their dark waves until he had disobeyed God and was a poor rejected king, trying to maintain what the Lord had taken away from him.

How careful ought we be. All of us have weaknesses of character, defects of disposition, and a proneness to this sin or that. For one it is greed—we all steal from God, as many of us are doing. For another it is ambition—we all stab a brother or sister in the back in order to get ahead. For another it is drink, or sex, or laziness, or lying, or talebearing. We must pray daily:

> "Arm me with jealous care,
>   As in thy sight to live,
> And O thy servant, Lord, prepare
>   A strict account to give."

I have but a moment to tell you what was most ruinous and destructive in the failure of Saul. The memorial tells it: "He inquired not of the LORD." On an awful night before a fateful battle Saul and his troops camped on the northern ridge of Gilboa with a greater host of the Philistines on the other side of the valley. As night fell before the day of battle this poor, driven king saw the campfires of the Philistines and heard the murmur and banter of the Philistine troops joking and laughing before the morrow's fight. Samuel, his mentor, was dead. Saul should have talked with God that night. Instead, he disguised himself, pulled his cloak about him and slipped down the slopes of Gilboa until he came to the half-heathen village of Endor. There he inquired of a woman supposedly gifted with secret, occult, magic powers. And Samuel appeared, not at her bidding, but at God's command.

Saul heard no good word. The next day, the host of Philistines swept across the valley, and one commentator has imagined that the blood of Saul's soldiers flowed in defeat until the fountain of Jezreel ran red with blood all ten miles to the Jordan. The ranks of Israel were broken, her soldiers were slain, and that night Saul lay a corpse along with his sons. Thus the lament of Israel's sweetest singer: "The beauty of Israel is slain upon thy high places! . . . Ye mountains of Gilboa, let there be no dew, neither let there be rain, upon you, nor fields of offerings: for there the shield of the mighty is vilely cast away, the shield of Saul, as though he had not been anointed with oil. . . . How are the mighty fallen in the midst of the battle!"

And thus the epitaph: "So Saul died for his transgression which he committed against the LORD, even against the word of the LORD, which he kept not. . . . He inquired not of the LORD." Saul needed not to come to such an end. He had God and he had Samuel. He threw his chance away. Day by day he sank into ruin.

We have less reason for such an end and such a memorial. We have Jesus Christ to make everything so much clearer.

The Christian preacher must not strain to make the Christ event explicit in every sermon. Where it is at all reasonable to state it, one ought. This accounts for a part of the conclusion.

He stands, does our Lord, as the tallest of the Sons of Men and something infinitely more. His was the only completely sane life ever lived on this planet. He was not awed by authority nor bored by dullness nor repelled by disease nor scornful in the presence of sin. He turned the ugliest of circumstances into ineffable beauty and then at last made death bow to his will. The centuries come up to him, break ranks into an antiphony of "Before" and "After." Can we believe other than that the force that is in history is the force that is in him? We may study others, but Christ studies us. We may question creeds, but this Christ questions us.

For my part, I trust it all to him—my hope, my life, my care, my keeping, my soul, my eternal destiny.

The final paragraph is personal testimony, something of which we are all too afraid. The rest is admonition and promise.

And so we may live the days of our years sure that in Christ Jesus the way will grow brighter and brighter until that day which knows not dawn or dusk. In him, the memorial, nay, the eternal commendation of those who live forever in his presence, can be, "Well done, thou good and faithful servant."

NOTES

1. Brevard S. Childs, *Introduction to the Old Testament as Scripture* (Fortress Press, 1979), p. 80.

2. Werner Lemke, "The Synoptic Problem in Chronicler's History," *Harvard Theological Review,* Vol. 58 (1965), pp. 349–363.

3. James A. Sanders, *Torah and Canon* (Fortress Press, 1972), pp. 108–109.

7
Shaping Sermons by the Encounter of Text with Preacher

Thomas H. Troeger

FORMING THE SERMON

The most important shape for a preacher to remember is the shape of the listener's heart and soul and mind and strength. What shape are they in at the beginning of the sermon and what shape at the end?

Note that I did not simply say the listener's mind. That is the weakness of a lot of preaching: we remember the listener's mind but not the other faculties of personhood which are equally vital components of our God-given identity. "The marvel of man's bodily appearance is not at all to be excepted from the realm of God's image. This was the original notion, and we have no reason to suppose that it completely gave way, in P's theological reflection, to a spiritualizing and intellectualizing tendency. Therefore, one will do well to split the physical from the spiritual as little as possible: the whole man is created in God's image."[1] It follows that preaching which does not engage the whole person is theologically incomplete.

When I read a biblical text I open myself to how the words grasp my entire being, my entire image of God. I have discovered that words do more than signify and interpret. Words vibrate with tremors of past experience and present anxiety; they etch visions in the mind; they call up smells and sounds; they constrict the intestines with fear; they fill the head with lightness. Words have a kinesthetic and emotional as well as intellectual impact on listeners. If we ignore the material effect of language, we shall miss how

God is addressing all of who we are, all of who God has made us to be.

In a similar fashion the shape of a biblical text frequently communicates something more than a message from one mind to another. It may represent an experience that splurted and surged through the total human self of the writer. The text may tremble with the event from which it was born and tell us how the writer's heart and soul and mind and strength were refashioned.

Therefore, engaging the whole person for God requires something more than asking, What does the text mean? That is a significant question, but we must not restrict meaning to rational categories. "The meaningful character of all meaning cannot be wholly explained by an appeal to the fact that man is a conscious being, a being endowed with reason. Ultimately we will have to say: I happen to be constituted in such a way that watching a sun-lit world, a tasty meal, the company of friends, listening to a brilliant discourse or beautiful music, and arriving at understanding are full of meaning for me."[2]

I read a biblical text watching for where the sun is shining, helping myself to bread and wine if it's being served, joking with my ancient friends, and even getting up and dancing to the music if any is played. I expand the question of meaning beyond the boundaries of rationality by asking, What does the passage make me want to do?

Clap my hands and sing?

Get on my knees and pray?

Write my congressional representative?

And how is God reshaping me through the text?

By speaking through a metaphor that sends a rush of hope to my heart?

By telling a story that shines a searchlight on my life?

By touching my wounds and filling me with strength?

We preachers are tempted to avoid these questions. Focusing on the message that we have extracted from the passage, we can escape an encounter with the Word who is greater than all the print in our Bibles and all the pronouncements from our pulpits. We become gnostics, thinking we are saved by our knowledge rather than our faith. And our sermon outlines reveal the distance we have kept between God and ourselves. They are rational constructions that convey a lot of information but not the Word become flesh. Before they consult any commentaries or other Bible aids, the first thing preachers need to do is immerse themselves in the text, not in order to figure out what they want to say to others, but in order to hear what God has to say to them. Preachers cannot expect to change the listener's heart and soul and mind and strength when their own have not been touched.

I recall an English teacher who used to warn us never to read the critics on a poem until we had read and lived with the text ourselves. Otherwise we would rob ourselves of a raw encounter with the work. The same principle applies to Scripture. The first act of sermon preparation is to read and live with the biblical passage—listening, seeing, feeling how God is reshaping us through the text.

I now share the process of my living and working with the passage from which I shall be preaching, Jer. 1:4–10. Lynn Nelson, a former student, has asked me to deliver her ordination sermon and has indicated that this text has been central to her own sense of call. I have spent over an hour talking with Lynn about her ordination and about the congregation, a lively country town parish in upstate New York, who will be gathered to hear the sermon. Although at this point I shall be the primary listener to the text, the congregation is already present in my mind and influencing me at unconscious levels. It is impossible for me to approach Jeremiah's call with a blank mind, because the narrative does not exist as some pure tale independent of those who read it. "A story lives in relation to its tellers and its receivers; it continues because people want to hear it again, and it changes according to their tastes and needs."[3] In what follows, the tastes and needs of the congregation and myself are present because I am listening to how the text speaks to us as the particular people we are. Later in the exegesis I shall use the insights of commentators to expand, correct, and illumine my reading, but now is the hour for a meeting between God, Jeremiah and me.

I sit in the living room with a cup of hot coffee. It is early in the morning, no cars on the streets. I have been silent for several minutes, praying sometimes with words and thoughts and sometimes with nothing but the emptiness of my own being, waiting for God. An "Amen" arises in a whisper through my lips. It is not a conscious piece of speech but as though some visitor suggested we shift the conversation to a new topic and a new tone. I get up and put on a recording of some Handel concerti, favorites of mine for the warmth of the strings and the alternating moods of ebullience and grief. Like Saul depending on David's harp, I find music an invocation of the Spirit.

Although I will be focusing on vs. 4–10, I read through all of Jeremiah 1 to be clear about the context. I then lift my eyes from the text to let my head fill with the visions that have been touched off by Jeremiah's graphic language: a human embryo in a womb, the smell of almonds, a pot boiling over and acrid smoke, cities of bronze and cities lying in rubble. I do not hasten to organize these into a pattern or to focus on one or the other. Instead, I let them drift like the phantoms of a daydream upon the surface of my consciousness. The mythic-poetic shapes will link me up with associative chains of language and experience that lie within me. Hidden from immediate awareness, these patterns may reveal the interior witness of the Spirit. I write nothing. I say nothing. As the images fade I attend for a minute to the music. The French horns, like heaven's trumpets, announce it is time to return to the text.

"Now the word of the LORD came to me saying . . ." I picture a Word coming to me, floating in the air like a letter mailed down through some slot in heaven's box. The edge of the paper is aimed toward my eyes. When I rise to look down on the sheet and read the word, it disappears. I wonder: How does God's word come to Jeremiah? I think of the teenagers in the youth fellowship who used to ask me: "What does the Bible mean when God speaks to people—is it an actual voice that they could hear? Did you hear a voice like that when you became a minister?" I feel myself resisting their question for its naiveté and simplicity. But then I am filled with admiration for their honesty. What could be more natural than to wonder how God speaks to people? I find myself thinking: How did it happen, Jeremiah? How did God's word come to you? This better be good, Jeremiah, or my youth fellowship won't believe you—and neither will I.

I return to the text:

> "Before I formed you in the womb I knew you,
> and before you were born I consecrated you."

A picture of the amniotic sack, webbed with veins and red and containing an embryo, fills my mind. Although Jeremiah lived before the invention of intrauterine photography, I do not, and there is no way I can read these words without remembering a movie that shows the time-lapsed development of a human embryo. When the movie was over I wanted to drop on my knees and repeat, "Thank you, God, thank you, God," and I had a friend who said he thought we should have sung the Doxology. Now as I sit in my living room reshowing the film on the screen of my cranium I fill with tears of gratitude for the simple fact of being. I listen to a largo, awestruck that I should exist to receive such beauty. And in this moment of wonder I am no longer puzzled by the phrase, "Now the word of the LORD came to me saying," for the word of the Lord has come to me on my couch with a cup of coffee in my hand and Handel's concerti playing and my reading,

> "Before I formed you in the womb I knew you,
> and before you were born I consecrated you;
> I appointed you a prophet to the nations."

Nations!

Nations?

The word rattles me out of my mood and tender wonder. I had not read this far before because I had gotten carried away with the image of the womb.

Nations.

At the end of the couch is yesterday's *New York Times* with a headline on violence in Poland between the police and the labor union, Solidarity, and possible intervention by the Soviets. A chain of associations crystallizes in my mind:

Nations,
Auschwitz,
Tanks-over-bodies-crushed,
Nuclear war.

I record the words here vertically, because that is how they appear inside me, like a ladder lowered into the caverns of the mind, each step down bringing me past another layer of fear. I try to climb back up the ladder and escape to my earlier heights of wonder, but I find my mind frozen to attention.

Nations.

I remain still, listening to the music but finding no comfort in it. I do not read the next verse too soon. Just as I took time to celebrate the joy of God's creating me, so too I must face the terror of what God is saying.

At last I read Jeremiah's response: "Then I said, 'Ah, Lord GOD! Behold, I do not know how to speak, for I am only a youth.' " Good for you, Jeremiah! I don't blame Jeremiah one bit. His excuse strikes me as sound, and I join him in talking back to the Lord: "Go pick on Brezhnev, God. Or tell what you want to the President. But don't send your hardest word to Jeremiah—he's only a youth—and don't send it to me. I am just a middle-aged, middle-class preacher." I sit reflecting on how crazy God is, asking the young and the powerless to call the world to justice.

My record changer clicks off and the sound snaps me out of my reverie on God's response to Jeremiah:

> "But the LORD said to me,
> 'Do not say, "I am only a youth";
> for to all to whom I send you you shall go,
> and whatever I command you you shall speak.
> Be not afraid of them,
> for I am with you to deliver you,
>   says the LORD.' "

The air is still. I reread God's response to Jeremiah, this time aloud and slowly. Each word fills the room. After a word passes my lips, it expands and presses against the walls, the floor, and the ceiling, so there is no space left for my excuses. The room is filled with nothing but the whole, clean truth of God. I am ready to finish reading the passage.

"Then the LORD put forth his hand and touched my mouth; and the LORD said to me . . ." I reach my left hand up to my mouth and move the pads of my fingers gently across my lips. Since part of Jeremiah's receiving these words includes the sensation of his mouth being touched, I need to be kinesthetically engaged to get the full force of the passage. God is speaking not just to my mind but to my physical being as well, to the entire image of God. I read the rest of God's call alternating the words with a tap of my fingers upon my lips.

> "Behold, *(tap)* I *(tap)* have *(tap)* put *(tap)*
>   my *(tap)* words *(tap)* in *(tap)* your *(tap)* mouth *(tap)*.
> See, *(tap)* I *(tap)* have *(tap)* set *(tap)* you *(tap)*
>   this *(tap)* day *(tap)* over *(tap)* nations *(tap)*
>   and *(tap)* over *(tap)* kingdoms *(tap)*;
> to pluck up *(tap)* and *(tap)* to break down *(tap)*,
> to destroy *(tap)* and *(tap)* to overthrow *(tap)*,
> to build *(tap)* and *(tap)* to plant *(tap)*."

When I finish I sit exhausted, as if I have been wrestling with someone I love, often wanting to pull the person toward me in an embrace and other times wanting to get up and run free. Several minutes of utter silence—no thoughts, no images, no feelings, no message for Sunday's congregation, only the absolute certainty that God is with me, with me, with me, with me . . .

Finally an "Amen" arises in a spontaneous whisper through my lips. I go out to the kitchen, where I pour myself another cup of coffee and get my note pad and pencil. When I return, I put on a Haydn symphony. The pristine classical structure of his music sets a different tone and hooks the logical side of my mind. Although my preparation and delivery follow the existential dynamics of God's word, the rational functions of intelligence are indispensable to organizing a sermon. To neglect these gifts would be to distort the image of God every bit as much as when we ignore the noncognitive aspects of our personhood.

Up to this point I have not written a single word. I have only tried to open myself to God's Word as it has been brought to me through Jeremiah's call. Rather than write down an outline for a sermon or a theme or topic, I try to outline my experience *as it was shaped by the biblical text.* I reread the passage slowly to recall what happened to me and to create a structure other than the pure subjectivity of my experience. I limit myself to one word for each stage of my response to the text. This forces a hard-edged outline to emerge:

Skepticism
Recognition
Wonder
Fear
Resistance
Overpowered
Presence

My encounter with the text has been a conversation between God and Jeremiah, God and me. God has gripped my heart and mind and soul and strength and moved me from skepticism to an assurance of the divine presence.

I now have a basic shape for the sermon derived from the text. The sermon will help people identify and respond to God's call in their own lives. It will work through the tangled process of skepticism and resistance to an assurance of God's presence that will empower them to carry out God's command in the world. This assurance will come through an experiential appropriation of God's promise, "I am with you to deliver you."

I will deal with the modern skepticism as represented in the youth fellowship through imaginative narration. I know from my conversation with the ordinand, Lynn Nelson, that the teenagers' question about how God calls people is very alive for her congregation. As Urban T. Holmes III puts the matter: "Contemporary man does not discern in his experience any data that points to the sacred or transcendent. His filters are secularized."[4] This was not a problem for Jeremiah, but it is for my contemporary listeners, and I cannot afford to ignore it and concentrate only on the message of God's promise. Thus, not only the text will shape the sermon but also the modern consciousness of the listeners. The sermon will not come "straight from the Bible." It will come crooked from the Bible, bent into a new shape by the Spirit who is at work in my listeners' lives, though they have difficulty seeing that. The sermon will open the congregation to God's call by engaging the imaginative and metaphoric capacities that have atrophied through their reliance on a naive scientism.

Jeremiah has taken me into God's presence in the same way that a poet takes me to places I otherwise would never go and Bach leads me to heaven's gate and Picasso gets me to see lines and depths that before escaped my attention. These artists expand my powers of perception, so that when I tap on life's surface it sounds like a kettledrum instead of a coffee can. Now I shall follow their example and reactivate those media of the imagination through which the congregation may hear the divine resonance in their experience. I will be modifying Jeremiah's original meaning. Although the text is shaping my experience, I am also shaping the message according to where I feel the Spirit leading. This for me is part of the meaning of the traditional formula: "There is always more light to break forth from God's word."

The Text / JEREMIAH 1:4–10
EXEGETICAL OBSERVATIONS

In addition to various translations and study Bible notes, two commentaries provide particularly good information for this text: John Bright's *Jeremiah* and J. A. Thompson's *The Book of Jeremiah*. [5]

In dealing with this passage, the commentaries pay considerable attention to the Hebrew word *na'ar* (v. 6), which the RSV renders "youth," the NEB renders "child," and both Bright and Thompson translate "boy." It is important for any sermon on this text to note, therefore, that Jeremiah had a legitimate human excuse to protest God's call: he *was* young to speak to the nations in the name of the Lord.

But the exegetical observation that is most germane to our theme of sermon shapes is Bright's comment:

The call's salient features are: Jeremiah's awareness that he had been predestined for the prophetic office since before his birth; the overruling of his objections and the promise of divine aid; and the placing of the divine word in his mouth. This last is extremely important. The prophet understood himself quite literally as the mouthpiece of Yahweh, the messenger who reported what he had heard Yahweh say in the heavenly council (cf., e.g., xxiii 16–22).[6]

As I read this, I copy Bright's outline onto my sheet of paper, giving a line to each part of the call and comparing it to my outline. I underline "the placing of the divine word in his mouth" and make a note to myself: Sermon climax?

Two word and image studies move the sermon beyond my subjectivity into an appreciation of the phenomenological and historical world of Jeremiah himself. Verse 11 in the NEB is translated: "The word of the LORD came to me: 'What is it that you see, Jeremiah?' 'An almond in early bloom,' I answered." Thus the image is of a blossoming tree. The footnote in the Oxford Study Edition explains a wordplay between "almond" and the word "watch" in v. 12. Almonds are described and pictured in Bible dictionaries as having pink-white flowers and oblong, delicately veined leaves. In one picture the leaves peek gently between the full petals of the blossoms, giving some idea of what Jeremiah himself must have seen. We know from Ex. 25:32–38 that the candlestick cups in the Temple were designed after almond blossoms. Although v. 11 is not formally a part of the call passage, this small detail supplies a visual feeling for Jeremiah's world and the nonverbal ways God's word came to him.

In addition, Thompson provides a fascinating word study on the Hebrew word *hiṣṣil,* which the RSV translates "deliver" and which Thompson renders "rescue." "If Jeremiah knew the Exodus story, and there is every reason to believe he did, he would have known that Yahweh 'rescued' his people from Egypt. But the verb was used in other well-known narratives, e.g., the rescue of David from the paw of a bear or a lion (I Sam. 17:37), and was employed in the songs sung in temple services with a much wider meaning than mere physical deliverance."[7]

Both Bright and Thompson comment that Jeremiah was probably raised in a pious home, which gives something of a feel for Jeremiah's childhood and the forces that might have prepared him to receive a word from the Lord: visions of the Temple and tales of a young man who slew lions and giants in the name of God.

As I put all of this together, I decide that this sermon will be a dialogue between God and Jeremiah, God and Us. I shall tell the story of Jeremiah's call so that it takes place simultaneously in ancient and modern times, in 627 B.C. and in our own day. I can do this through a variety of technical devices: I can employ phrases and vocal inflections that are part of common speech patterns to contemporize Jeremiah's call. I can act out portions of the story with simple gestures that will draw the congregation into an experience of the immediacy of Jeremiah's call. I can ignore the usual grammatical rules for change of tense when I move between Jeremiah's and the congregation's experience so that listeners do not receive the prophet's call as something locked up back in biblical days. All of these devices represent more than mere technique. They are part of a strategy to make the retelling of Jeremiah's story an event in which the congregation hears God's call to them. "Recent writers have tended to emphasize that the biblical memory is not merely theoretical—i.e., the recalling of an objective memory image—but that it recalls conditions and determines the behavior of him who remembers. But to a certain extent this is true also of the most intimate, personal, and religious memories of modern man. It is as well to know that for the Hebrew the recollection of the past means that *what is recalled becomes a present reality,* which in turn controls the will."[8]

Sometimes when I preach I use illustrations to help what is recalled become a present reality, but for this particular sermon, I am going to focus on the experience of Jeremiah, using the biblical story simultaneously as the modern story. There will be no precise distinction between the biblical exposition and the application to the listeners' lives. All will flow together in one integrated event. I do not take such an approach in every sermon, but I am led to it this time by two factors: Lynn Nelson's telling me how intrigued and baffled many congregation members are by the idea

of God's calling someone; and by the vivid contemporaneity of
Jeremiah's story that I have experienced in preparing this sermon.
These are more than rational considerations, although they are, to
be sure, at least that. These are for me the promptings of the Spirit
who speaks through the total process of my preparation.

I break the passage into natural sections of dialogue. I am overpowered by a vision of the sermon. Here it comes!

Sermon / I AM WITH YOU

Jeremiah sat down under the almond tree, drawing his knees
beneath his chin and curling his feet into the soil. He was glad to
have his parents off his back. While the gumdrop sun melted in
the west, he looked at the branches above his head and pretended
they were the rafters of a house, a place of his own where there
were no demands. The rose twilight filtered through the pink-
white blossoms, so that the canopy of flowers blended with the
soft shining of heaven.

*The details of feet in the soil, blossoms, and evening light are to
help the listeners feel how God's word comes to flesh-and-blood
people like themselves. The materiality of the language engages
the whole image of God as I have discussed it in my opening
essay.*

Jeremiah's eyes traced the tender leaves, oblong and veined like
the wings of the cherubim that decorated the Temple in Jerusalem.
For a moment Jeremiah felt free from lessons, free from chores,
free from time.

Jer—e—miiiii—ah!

*The vocal inflection of the prophet's name—an elongated cre-
scendo and decrescendo—will become an integrating theme in
the sermon. It will draw on the listeners' childhood memories,
their relationship to their human parents and the heavenly par-
ent.*

Mom, he thought, was calling him home for supper. Jeremiah pressed his spine against the trunk and his feet into the soil, wedging himself into his private world. The memory of adult voices gusted through his mind, and he found himself back in his parents' house at the supper table. His uncle was ripping the air with angry words: "I'm telling you the Assyrians are going to get theirs now. Babylon is rising up, and that is what we've got to deal with. If it means an alliance with Egypt, so be it. But we cannot have a do-nothing foreign policy. Let's make Israel great again."

I give the historical setting through an angry supper conversation in order to set off contemporary political reverberations.

Jeremiah's father responded in the same fiery tone: "I still say the best foreign policy is security at home. Ever since Manasseh things have been rotten in Jerusalem. I don't want us to put all that money into the defense establishment. It's time for reform in the capital. We've got to get our national priorities straight. Josiah is open to that; we've got to give him a chance."

I have lifted some of the language about politics out of presidential campaigns in order to connect with listeners' political sensibilities. Without telling the congregation how to vote, I am affirming that God's call comes to Jeremiah, comes to them, in a time of political turmoil.

Jeremiah stared at a single almond blossom, trying to still the angry voices within him by concentrating on the sepals and petals of the flower. He noted they looked like the cups on the candelabra in the Temple and remembered the priest quoting Moses' directions for the menorah: "Three cups made like almonds, each with capital and flower, on one branch."

Jeremiah's association of the leaves and the Temple candelabra is an imaginative development of Bright's claim that we can assume Jeremiah was brought up in a home of traditional piety. This may help the congregation see how religious education has a role in opening us to the mystery of God's call.

A wind swept across the fields, and Jeremiah twisted his face around because he thought he heard someone climbing up into the tree. Or was it down into the tree? The oblong leaves began to flutter and the air was filled with cherubim, their wings humming holiness into the atmosphere. The trunk of the tree became the central shaft of a menorah and the branches became the side stems. The blossoms turned darker red until they were tongues of flame.

Jer—e—miiiii—ah!

Again the voice, like his mother's, yet not his mother's, came from beyond him, yet inside him. Words expanded inside Jeremiah like the unfurling of an embryo in time-lapsed photography, each syllable increasing the body of truth that was developing within him:

The image of the embryo is a modern scientific one, unknown to Jeremiah, but it has the same spirit of wonder that the biblical verse conveys. The cinemagraphic updating of the ancient words is an attempt to show the congregation how God is calling through the wonders that science reveals to them.

> "Before I formed you in the womb I knew you,
> and before you were born I consecrated you;
> I appointed you a prophet to the nations."

I read the words of the text very slowly, and gently extend my hands and arms outward, as though I am the embryo that is uncoiling. The rhythm of the words, the body language, and the metaphor become an integrated expression of Jeremiah's dawning awareness.

The humming of holiness pressed against Jeremiah's eardrums in waves of increasing intensity. Jeremiah turned his head to survey the galaxy of flame and cherubim that gleamed and fluttered above him. He found himself in God's heavenly council. Out of Jeremiah's throat came a voice that was his but did not sound like himself:

"Ahhhhh, Lord GOD!"

Then the boy paused, the same pause he used with his parents when they asked him to do an errand and he did not want to. Two of God's words, brittle and sharp like almond shells, rattled against each other inside Jeremiah:

Womb Nations.

I highlight the words to evoke in listeners chains of associations in the subconscious: womb—warmth—escape; nations—violence—fear. The unspoken connotations can increase the intuitive identification with Jeremiah's struggle.

He wanted the shell of the womb to shatter the shell of the nations.

Jeremiah closed his eyes and pretended the tree was only a tree and the blossoms were only blossoms and the leaves were only leaves. He pretended he was curled beneath a leafy green tree in paradise and the sun was shining pink and white and warm. But when he opened his eyes the cherubim were still there, and they beat their wings even harder, and the pulsations of air carried God's words to Jeremiah over and over:

"I appointed you a prophet to the nations.
I appointed you a prophet to the nations."

The double reversal—Jeremiah's pretending the tree is only a tree—is an attempt to help listeners release their choking grip on the world of appearances, to unclog the filters of their secular consciousness. It is a way of stressing the reality of Jeremiah's encounter with God.

The air cracked, like the snap of a nutshell between two rocks, and the only word whose point scratched the air was: nations, nations, nations.

Jeremiah leaped up and grabbed the lowest stem of the candelabra. "Behold, I do not know how to speak, for I am only a youth. My uncle and father do not even listen to me. The world will never hear me!" Then Jeremiah shook the menorah with all his might, trying to overturn it and burn God's palace down.

*The scene provides an opportunity for the listeners to own their
rebellion against God. Unless this is acknowledged, the decision
to obey God may come from the mouth but not from the heart.
(Cf. Matt. 21:28–32.)*

Jeremiah collapsed, sobbing on the earth.

Then stillness.

When Jeremiah looked up he saw again the canopy of almond
leaves and blossoms above him. The evening air was growing
colder, but inside his body he felt a strange warmth: the flames
that had leaped from the candlestand were not burning inside his
bones. Once more Jeremiah heard the voice, but this time it was
much closer, as if his mother had come to stand over his bed after
they had had an argument. She was not going to give in, but she
was going to speak closely and tenderly, explaining how Jeremiah
could do what he thought he could not.

*The shift between God in heaven and God like his mother over
his bed is an expression of Jeremiah's theology that God is both
"at hand" and "afar off." (Cf. Jer. 23:23ff.)*

> "Do not say, 'I am only a youth';
>   for to all to whom I send you you shall go,
>   and whatever I command you you shall speak.
> Be not afraid of them,
>   for I am with you to deliver you,
>   says the LORD."

Deliver.

The word hooked a favorite memory inside of Jeremiah and
he found himself again at the supper table with his uncle and
father, but this time there were no angry voices. His father and
uncle were full and mellow and telling favorite stories. Jeremiah's uncle was playing the role of Saul, and Jeremiah's father
was David, explaining to the king why he would fight Goliath:
" 'The LORD who delivered me from the paw of the lion and
from the paw of the bear, will deliver me from the hand of this
Philistine.' "

Here again, I try to take seriously the influence of Jeremiah's religious background. I want the congregation to pull on their own memories of first hearing the Bible stories so that they can appreciate how God has been shaping them through Scripture and tradition for many years.

Jeremiah imagined himself as David and jumped to his feet, picking up a stone that lay next to him and pretending it was the rock he would sling to kill the giant. Leaves from the lowest branch of the almond tree brushed across his face. Their touch startled him, and he stood still. A single oblong leaf flapped gently against his lips, like a finger tapping a message in code.

I stop speaking and tap my right index finger against my lips for several seconds. The silence and the gesture communicate the nonverbal mystery of God's coming to us without gabbing about it.

Jeremiah pushed the branch to the side and stepped away from the tree. When he let go of the branch it whipped back into position, and in the swishing of the leaves Jeremiah heard once more the same tender but implacable voice:

> "Behold, I have put my words in your mouth.
> See, I have set you this day over nations
>   and over kingdoms,
> to pluck up and to break down,
> to destroy and to overthrow,
> to build and to plant."

Jeremiah gulped. Again he heard his uncle and father talking. This time his father was quoting Deuteronomy: "I will raise up for them a prophet like you from among their brethren; and I will put my words in his mouth, and he shall speak to them all that I command him."

Jeremiah reached his hand back over his shoulder and hurled the rock across his father's fields.

I hurl an imaginary stone out of the pulpit through a glass window and wait for it to land in the town streets outside. This gesture of high physical energy is a way of saying that God has empowered Jeremiah without using that cliché. I stare out of the window—the stone has been hurled from 627 B.C. into November 1980. I notice that some congregation members look to see where it has landed: in the streets of the village where they live. This is exactly what I am after, bringing the story of Jeremiah's call to life in their own place and time.

He watched for where it landed, but by now it was too dark to see anything but the hills silhouetted against the last lingering of light. He pursued their outline of angles and slopes, and they seemed to him like city walls, battered and broken. Jeremiah stood surveying the destroyed city until the blackness of the ruins and the blackness of the night were one.

Jeremiah took a deep breath of the cool air and stepped toward home. He knew the way well, but it seemed as though the world were rearranged beneath his feet, and every four steps pushed up these words from the earth:
I AM WITH YOU.
I AM WITH you.
I AM with you.
I am with you.

I start the first sentence in a loud voice but decrescendo to a pianissimo by the last repeat. This creates the illusion of Jeremiah's walking away and also echoes the many different ways God calls people: from a shout to a whisper.

While Jeremiah walks home to the beat of God's promise, sit beneath your own almond tree and listen for the voice that calls you.

The shift to the present tense maintains the simultaneity of ancient and contemporary time.

Lynn—Nelllll—son!
Cor—fuuuuu—New York!

Both names are inflected the same as "Jeremiah" was earlier. The vocal similarity draws on the experience of Jeremiah's call so that the listeners can appropriate his story to illumine their own lives.

From here on I follow the dialogue pattern of the prophet's call. The parallelism is meant to pull the congregation into conversation with God.

However, I deliberately do not raise up illustrations of modern prophets. I do not want to overwhelm the listeners with heroic examples that seem beyond their reach. I believe that God calls each of them in some way and that if I can help them hear that call through an imaginative engagement with Jeremiah's experience I shall have accomplished my major goal.

We have heard this voice. We have heard it like Jeremiah. We were retreating into our private world when a voice—a prompting of the heart, an ache in the conscience, a call from within yet beyond—unsettled our daydream world of no demands.

And how have we responded? Like Jeremiah! The first words out of our mouth were:

I am too young.
Or
I am too old.
Or
I am middle-aged, caring for the old and raising the young.
Or
I am just a solitary individual. What difference can I make?

But God says to us what God said to Jeremiah: "Do not say, 'I am too young or too old or too middle-aged or too solitary.' I am with you to deliver you. I am with you in your words. I am with you in your actions. I am with you whenever you take a stand for what is good and true and right and just."

Rather than persuade people to serve God, I depend on God and God's promise. If through the drama of Jeremiah's call, they feel God with them, that single fact will make more difference than hours of argument for why they should get involved.

We may all be tongue-tied prophets, but we serve an eloquent God. That is what Jeremiah discovered. He would have been glad to sit under that almond tree, to retreat into his private little world. And sometimes in his ministry he did retreat. He would decide not to say another word about God. But then he would discover:

> "There is in my heart as it were a burning fire
>   shut up in my bones,
>   and I am weary with holding it in,
>   and I cannot."

Jeremiah blazed with a truth greater than his private world. And if you've ever known a word of love that you had to speak, if you've ever tasted a word of justice that you had to do, if you've ever danced with a word of joy that you had to share, then you too have blazed with a truth greater than your private world. It is the truth that burns like fire in your bones, the truth that makes the same promise to you that was made to Jeremiah:

Again I eschew argument for an attempt to help people draw the experiential connection between the prophet's call and their own lives. I assume God is already at work with them and they need help in identifying the hidden motions of the Spirit.

I AM WITH YOU.
I AM WITH you.
I AM with you.
I am with you.

I end the congregation's call the same way I ended Jeremiah's: by repeating God's promise from a shout to a whisper. That promise sustained Jeremiah through his ministry, and it will do the same for the new pastor and her congregation.

The entire sermon has been an effort not just to tell people the truth but to help them feel it brushing against the inside walls of their hearts.

NOTES

1. Gerhard von Rad, *Genesis, A Commentary,* The Old Testament Library (Westminster Press, 1961), p. 56.

2. Remy C. Kwant, *Phenomenology of Language* (Duquesne University Press, 1965), p. 22.

3. Marina Warner, *Joan of Arc: The Image of Female Heroism* (Alfred A. Knopf, 1981), p. 3.

4. Urban T. Holmes III, *Ministry and Imagination* (Seabury Press, 1976), p. 55.

5. John Bright, *Jeremiah* (Doubleday & Co., 1965); J. A. Thompson, *The Book of Jeremiah* (Wm. B. Eerdmans Publishing Co., 1980).

6. Bright, *Jeremiah,* pp. 6–7.

7. Thompson, *The Book of Jeremiah,* p. 149.

8. George Arthur Buttrick (ed.), *The Interpreter's Dictionary of the Bible,* Vol. 3 (Abingdon Press, 1962), p. 344 (italics mine).